ALL THAT I HAD

ALL THAT I HAD

Kathy Ann Corse

ISBN 978-0-578-48561-4 (softcover)
ISBN 978-0-578-57023-5 (kindle)
ISBN 978-0-578-57024-2 (EPUB)

Library of Congress Control Number:2019913114

Cover and interior design by Linda Parke
www.ravenbookdesign.com

Printed and bound in Canada
First Printing August, 2019

To my Mom.
Thank you, Mom, for giving me more than you needed to.
For doing more than you were asked to do. And for being all
that God called you to be with your beautiful
smile and sweet, loving spirit.

This true story was written as a tribute to my Mother who is one of the "richest" people I know and how she chose to live her one remarkable story. It is also dedicated to all readers who desire a simpler, slow-paced and meaningful existence and to discover through the story the value of what really matters most in life.

This book is an easy read. It is not one more thing to add to an already busy schedule, but instead is meant as an invitation for those who feel overwhelmed and rushed to step into peace, encouragement and a wonderful warm feeling. It will give you comfort in knowing that even the simplest acts of kindness can empower your life and the lives of those around you in ways you never dreamed possible!

Turn off the outside noises and take a trip back in time with me. The story is written in a fashion for readers to feel like they are right there. Smell the pot roast dinner, the fresh pine at the holidays and picture family together to "taste" what life was like. Hop into Grandpa's 1948 Hudson and snuggle in for a horse-drawn "Currier and Ives" sleigh ride! It was a time when people were busy, lacking all the modern conveniences we have today, yet they survived and often thrived. It was a time when people knew no different. It is a story of a woman who took what she had, combined it with love, strength and courage, and made the best of her life and those around her.

Memories of my Mother's love and generosity are many. Yet in 1960 one of her greatest acts of selflessness would affect others for a lifetime. In the story you will witness this ultimate act of giving return to her some 36 years later in a very unexpected and amazing way. One day I asked her why she chose to do what she did. Her reply, "It was all that I had." Thus, the title of the book came into being.

The impact of a parent's love and example can have a tremendous effect on children. Growing up, watching Mom, I didn't know any different. I thought that her focus on others was the norm until I became an adult. It was then that I realized what an exceptional quality she possessed. From generation to generation her special gift was quietly given with tenderness and compassion. Her life of service was so much better and richer than no life at all. She had her priorities right.

I made the decision years ago to follow in her footsteps and dedicate time to help family and friends, thus the story has taken me longer to write than I would have liked, but Mom would have it no other way. Every day is a blessing, so I call and read to her in the moment, as soon as more pages are written. The excitement in her voice and the enjoyment I've experienced while writing has taken this book from a dream to reality. As a single parent for many years, I appreciate the considerable challenges that people face today with lack of time. We all must make choices and sacrifices. Respect is key for those who "wear many hats" at the same time.

The writing of this book has been a desire for many years and holds a special place in my heart. It is a story that needed to be told and will serve a true purpose: to make readers smile, shed a tear or two and give real meaning to your life.

It has been an honor to write about someone for whom I have so much love and respect. She is my inspiration, role model and mentor. At the age of 96, Mom is still with us. You'll find her working at the local food pantry or serving a meal at the soup kitchen. Perhaps she's preparing a lesson for Sunday Church School or helping with Chucky, who you will hear about in the story. If it's a nice day, she'll pass you on her riding mower, tend to her bird feeders or head to a swim class at the local Y. And she's ready and willing to tell you all about her grandchildren, the loves of her life.

I can close my eyes and hear her whistling her way through the day, experience her warm, lively and enjoyable temperament and witness her positive effect on others wherever she goes!

It is my desire for each of you to find a relaxing place, settle in, and travel back in time with me. I hope you'll enjoy reading this book as much as I've enjoyed writing it!

Contents

Return to the Past

{A note from the author}

*D*ear Readers,
In the very beginning of the book, the main character introductions provide enough information so that you'll be able to visualize each individual. This is accomplished by giving detailed descriptions of the lead characters' physical attributes, personality traits and very importantly, upbringing.

A person's childhood can be strongly correlated with his actions as you will see how vastly different upbringings of the two main characters contributed to how they chose to react to life and live their lives. These early experiences can stay with us for years to come, shaping our future behavior well into adulthood. It all depends on what we choose to do. We are not doomed to repeat history. We can take lessons learned from our formative years, and choose to change or improve, while creating a more positive outcome for ourselves and for those we love and care about.

In addition, the setting or surroundings of the story are designed to picture the scenes as if you were present. With other characters added to the story, it's a great way to feel connected to the plot. While writing, readings were shared with my family. Their response was, "I can picture this!" or "I feel like I'm right there!"

Watch closely as the story unravels and the plot develops with details and emotion. This allows you to easily follow along from start to finish, as we turn back the clock and step back in time.

~ Kathy Ann Corse

Introduction

The smell of fresh cut grass filled the morning air, and after parking the mower she unloaded her garden tools in the corner of the garage and closed the door. Heading to the backyard, she filled each feeder with an abundance of seed, then made her way up the deck stairs to enjoy a rich cup of coffee. It was just 8am and her morning exercise was complete. She made every effort to keep in good shape: both physically and mentally. Today's cryptogram was finished, sitting next to her chair in the living room.

The woman took pride in whatever she did and her beautifully manicured lawn was no exception. Relaxing in a padded lawn chair, she'd need to pace herself today, as in just a few hours her work at the local food pantry would start. The arthritis pains she'd dealt with along with her recent surgery left her with a little less energy than usual. Other than that, the 96 year old was determined to continue her normal routine.

She gazed out over the yard, and memories of days gone by returned to her. She had had a good life, some years filled with challenges, yet they were overshadowed by the happier times.

As she closed her eyes and dozed, Catherine's vivid mind would revisit her past. The pictures and events were still clear, as she traveled back decades earlier in her life.

The Purchase

On February 4th, 1950, a man walked into a jewelry store in Newark, New Jersey to make a special purchase. It would be an engagement ring for the love of his life. As he knew this piece of jewelry would be worn for a lifetime, he took his time making the selection. The knowledgeable jeweler contributed in helping him choose the best diamond for her taste and for his requirements. This was not an easy task as every ring was made with superior craftsmanship and quality.

After much thought, the gentleman chose a lovely gold solitaire band with timeless style. It perfectly complimented the diamond which was elegant and simple. He was pleased to know this exquisite piece would be something she would treasure forever. After purchasing the ring for $175.00 and requesting it be beautifully gift wrapped, he left the store with the breathtaking ring. It would be a classic expression for the one true love he would share a lifetime with.

Selecting the perfect ring and the upcoming engagement was just the start of many things to come in their life together.

Yet, little did they know the journey this ring would take and the lives that would be changed forever by this compelling story.

Kenneth J. Corse II

enneth J. Corse II was born on December 30th, 1919 to Charles Jerome and Elizabeth Belle Corse of Boonton, New Jersey. His father was one of the first to graduate from Penn State's engineering program in 1910. His technical skills were impeccable and he'd settle for nothing less than outstanding work at all times. At home, he also expected his entire family to abide by these extremely high standards of professional achievement.

For Kenneth and his sister Eleanor, their upbringing was considered a happy one, yet these unrealistic goals put a great deal of pressure on the family. To please their father, excellence was not an option. The house was to be kept meticulously. Report cards brought home with anything other than A grades were deemed unacceptable.

Years passed and soon Ken graduated from Boonton High School. His senior quote was "his heart and hand, open and free." As a young man he won the hearts of many girls and enjoyed life as a bachelor. His education in Tool Design at the

Ken, 1948

local trade school landed him a secure job and a wonderful start to a long career.

At the age of 29, life was good for Kenneth. Success in his career as a tool designer continued. Days were filled reading blueprints and designing tools, engines and machines for the government. His drawings were impeccable, and Kenneth's employer was pleased with the quality of his superb work and his commitment to the job.

On weekends, Kenneth would spend time at the family cottage on Cranberry Lake, New Jersey- a vacation spot he cherished as a boy. Countless childhood memories of seasonal visitors kept him returning to this much-loved place. His favorite times were when family would arrive by way of Old Highway 31 in their Model T Fords. Also known as the "Tin Lizzie," these cars offered travel for many middle-class Americans. Other family members would travel on the Erie Lackawanna Railroad, whose station sat at the lake's eastern shore. On a busy weekend over a thousand visitors would arrive at the lake by way of train.

As a boy he looked forward to family picnics with his favorite foods of fresh fruit pies, chocolate layer cake, glazed pheasant, stuffed eggs and Parker House rolls. Along with all these tasty foods were heaps of fresh fruit and hard cheeses. Weekends were busy using his runabout boat, a gift his father had given him at the age of 12. It was small, fast and powerful and one of the few boats on the lake at that time equipped with a brand new Evinrude motor. The boat provided him with years of racing, fishing and water-skiing pleasure. He also gave lake tours to relatives and friends.

The family savored these gatherings and lifetime memories were created.

Cranberry Lake, 1930

Catherine Rose Shaffer

atherine Rose Shaffer was born on June 29th, 1923, the daughter of Orval Wesley and Ethel Rose Shaffer. As proud Pennsylvania Dutch, they were a culture formed by early German immigrants. The Shaffer family exemplified a strong work ethic and were pleased to call Bloomsburg home. Orval and Ethel had five children: Catherine, Jackie, Nadine, Orval Jr. and Richard. As Orval was responsible for a large family, he dug ditches during the depression to provide food for them. He also worked at the Bloomsburg brickyard, one of the largest suppliers of bricks in the area. Daily he was kept busy grinding clay and molding bricks. Other journeymen and young stone layers would work hand in hand to build many of the town homes, shops and stores with bricks made from the local yard.

Bloomsburg bricks represented beauty and historical permanence that would last for years to come. The brick streets and cobblestone pavers were built with such charm, character and craftsmanship that bricklaying was considered respectable manual labor. This skill required a degree of artfulness and Orval was proud of the work he did.

Orval was also employed by Jimmy Stradling, owner of the greenhouses on Light Street in Bloomsburg. His responsibilities included planting seeds and maintaining the growing greenhouse flowers. Firing up the boilers on cold days to keep the greenhouses warm was a task Orval enjoyed and often the children would come along to watch. Jimmy had a thriving floral business from the local hospital. Deliveries to patients consisted of gorgeous arrangements of yellow and pink roses, lilies and hypericum. Large accounts with the churches and funeral homes kept the business going and growing. Vases of pink carnations and white spider mums filled the delivery trucks as a traditional way of expressing condolences.

Orval embraced the Shaffer family history of a strong work ethic combined with integrity. He was punctual, put in his best effort and completed all the flower deliveries on time. These were some of the many qualities that kept him working with Jimmy for years. His love for gardening and flowers made the job enjoyable, while bringing a smile to work with him every day.

The hometown folks referred to him as "Bucky" and the nickname would follow him for the rest of his life. Bucky's optimistic outlook, generosity and friendly manner made him a likable person. People would greet him on the street with a warm hello. He and Ethel were well-respected in the community and the town folks looked out for them, and especially their children.

Character and integrity also extended into the home. It was helpful that Orval and Ethel were aligned with each other when it came to discipline. They were loving and consistent, realizing that obedience would be for their children's own good. With iron clad rules in effect, there were definite boundaries and consequences. The children were raised knowing they were loved and cared for while a strong message was sent as to what was right from wrong. One example was the number of times a baseball entered through the living room window, shattering the pane. After making several costly repairs, Orval replaced it for the last time using an old piece of glass found in the chicken coop. Silence speaks volumes. The window remained untouched for years to come.

They taught respect at an early age that encompassed all relatives including grandparents John and Katie Shaffer, who were held in high esteem by the family. It was routine that the children would stop at "Granny and Pappy's" house at lunchtime and on their daily walk home from school.

The boys loved to ride their bicycles and were given permission to travel to the school and playground. To Richard and Orval Jr. cycling represented fun and freedom. The balloon tires on their red Roadmasters rolled easily and the carefree biking often got them into some trouble as they were spotted downtown sailing across intersections and maneuvering the wrong way on Light Street. Word of mouth communication worked very well in those days, as the parents had a full report of the sightings before the family sat down for the evening meal.

Orval's parents, John and Katie Shaffer owned a large property on Glen Avenue and Franklin Street. Sitting at the bottom of the Franklin Street hill, their house was stately and distinguished, characterized by

John & Katie Shaffer, 1926

solid homeowners with traditional values. In those days, it was normal for many families to live nearby, so John parceled out a portion of land on Franklin Street for each of his children. The historical homes, built by John and Orval, had continuity that unified them aesthetically.

With members of multiple generations living near each other, the family became close knit while making it a point not to interfere. They leaned on each other, providing support. While the grandparents helped with the grandchildren, their own children would be there for them in their later years.

The children checked in on their grandmother on the way home from lunch and once again, after school. Affected with an eye disease that damaged her optic nerve, Granny's vision loss from glaucoma was gradual and progressive and finally left her permanently blind. Although she lost her sight, she still made every effort to keep busy with the homestead.

As long as she didn't confuse the salt and sugar, homemade cookies were ready after school-warm and delicious. Coming from a long line of cheerful whistlers, granddaughter Catherine's melody would signal their arrival to Granny. The children sat in the kitchen and chatted while eating their afternoon snack.

On special occasions the children were allowed to spend time in the parlor. Holding a prominent place on the coffee table was a well-worn book called: "Titanic." They flipped through the pages and gazed at the pictures of famous people on board the sinking ship, reading the story over and over again.

A Special Grandmother

Remember our own dear Granny
Who lived at the foot of the hill,
Though her frail body lies asleep there
She lives in memories still.

For in each of our hearts that Granny
Nicked out a little space,
And fitted it with fond memories
That time cannot erase.

Remember the quilts and aprons she made
And her big apple trees that gave us shade
As we slid down her cellar door?

And dresses with sparklers
Coats with fur
And warm night gowns that her hands fashioned
for us in love.

Remember in winter days cold and chill
How she insisted on helping us up the hill
with cookies made just for us.

Remember her sweet bread and molasses pie
And her snow on the mountain that grew so high
In the garden she tended with love.

And remember how she always said
When gathering up the crumbs of bread
"Give them to the birds, they will thank you with
a song."

After braving the years of darkness
Of living without her sight,
How happy she must be to suddenly
Behold that City of Light

~ Jackie Shaffer, June 22, 1958

~ *4* ~

Ethel Rose
and her Children

E thel Rose Shaffer was an extremely hard worker and of Scottish descent. At first impression, she might be considered reserved, yet after the first few meetings people would find her to be warm hearted, gregarious and a very friendly woman.

Ethel gave birth to seven children, all delivered by Dr. McKelvey, the Shaffer's family physician. Sadly, two of the children did not survive. The first baby, Dennis, was a full-term pregnancy, yet resulted in a stillbirth. The second infant was termed a "blue baby" at birth. Baby Phillip lacked oxygen in the blood and had a heart abnormality. With no found treatments or medical advances at the time, there was little chance for him to survive. This was a difficult and complex tragedy for Orval, Ethel, and their family.

Ethel Shaffer, 1941

For the Shaffers, and especially Ethel, not only did they lose two precious children they loved, there was also a loss of what might have been. The present was lost by the death of these children, but so was the future.

Naming both children actualized their worth and identity. Because they were valued and loved, memorial services were held for both babies. Their lives did matter. It was a sad time, yet the acknowledgment helped bring the family closure and assisted in the grieving of their precious losses.

In the years ahead, Ethel focused on her family and worked from home. With five children to care for, she led a busy life. Each Shaffer property consisted of a thriving and bountiful vegetable garden and she chose the south side of the house for planting as the area provided an abundance of sunshine. She was well aware that a healthy and productive garden would demand much time and attention. Because of Orval's long working hours, she had to enlist the help of her children.

It was rewarding to have this portion of the yard close by so she could enjoy the fruits of their labor. The garden was visited regularly. On a daily basis, weeds and pests were removed and aged manure was added. Tilling the dirt kept the plot well drained and the soil loose enough for the vegetables to thrive.

Ethel canned as many vegetables as possible so that the family could enjoy the bounty of the summer produce all year long.

Jackie, Catherine and Nadine picked and washed tomatoes, peas and string beans that went from the garden to the jar.

To keep the food from freezing during the winter and prevent spoilage during the summer, Orval and his two sons built a root cellar. The northeast foundation walls of the home provided two sides of the root cellar while the other two walls were built with stud and board. To keep the heat out, Orval Jr. and Richard insulated the interior walls and door, and installed a simple ventilation system. This allowed fresh air from outside to be brought into the root cellar as stale air was exhausted.

Stored vegetables consisted of carrots, turnips, beets, onions, parsnips and potatoes. Other stored supplies were preserves, jams and Ethel's homemade sassafras root beer. Served cold, this beverage was a hit during the family gatherings in the 1920s and 1930s. As friends and family sipped away, the story was told about how her famous root beer got started.

When walking one day, Ethel discovered a root beer fragrance and wild growing sassafras at the edge of the backyard where it met the wooded area. The small, bushy sassafras tree was found under the canopy of large apple trees. Making the nourishing and naturally fermented beverage became a family project, as the fragrance of sugar, molasses, wintergreen leaf, vanilla, cinnamon and allspice delighted the senses.

To brighten the winter months, concord grapes were picked from the arbor in the backyard. The smell of rich, ripe grapes was a reminder of Ethel's homemade grape juice. After washing and de-stemming the grapes, they were simmered in a large metal pot and strained through cheesecloth. Thick, smooth, nectar-like juice was ladled into glass jars to cool before being stored in the root cellar, while grape mash was composted in the garden.

From kindergarten through 12th grade, Ethel volunteered to help at school. She took a real interest in her children's education and felt that volunteering was a worthwhile cause.

Mouth-watering vanilla bean cupcakes with buttery frosting and citrus sugar cookies with lemon icing were some of the many sweet creations she packaged in tins and sent to school on a regular basis.

An iron treadle sewing machine made many a costume for Halloween and school plays. The purchase of a Singer model was an investment and Ethel was proud to have it sitting in the living room showcased in the Amish made cabinet. At night, she brought out her large sewing basket and spread the contents on the dining room table. Carefully, fabric was laid out, often muslin, which was selected for practicality and suitability.

A box of Butterick patterns was brought down from the attic for the children to look through. Coming in different sizes, patterns were printed on tissue paper, cut, folded and inserted into envelopes complete with instruction sheets. With the Great Depression affecting American families, spending was curtailed and more people than ever before were purchasing patterns and learning to sew at home. After much consideration, measurements were taken, styles were selected, and production started.

Meals for the family were cooked on a coal stove in the warm and inviting kitchen. The food was diverse and tasty, wholesome but not fancy. Porridge was a morning staple. A huge pot was prepared with a hint of cinnamon and nutmeg with a smell that spread through the entire house. The porridge then cooled and set before being sliced and eaten for breakfast or put in a sack and enjoyed later that day. Fresh eggs collected from the chicken coop were delicious with bright yolks and firm whites. Home baked biscuits with apple butter were waiting in the oven warmer to be enjoyed.

A Shaffer tradition was to gather the family together for an evening meal. Everything eaten came from the garden, root cellar, or pantry. "If you didn't grow it, you didn't eat it" was a popular saying in those days. Root vegetables, potatoes and carrots would show up in many savory dishes. Sunday dinner was special as beef or raised chicken was included in the meal. Dessert complemented Sunday dinner and every evening meal. Apples and rhubarb made wonderful pies and crumbles. Shoofly pie – rich in molasses and traditional among the Pennsylvania Dutch – was a highly enjoyable ending to a meal.

The children were taught to take turns clearing and setting the table using blue and white English china. Dinner plates featured a landscaped theme with a horse and cart, walkers along a stream and a floral and lattice border. Depression blue glasses were inexpensive yet pretty, and the vintage silver (which often required polishing), along with cloth napkins, completed the dinner table.

Although it took time and effort to keep these traditions, Orval and Ethel knew the family meal provided much needed structure in their children's lives. Dinner was a time to help them understand family values and morals, how to work in school and choose the right kind of friends. Added to the meal was the love and care put into it.

Another responsibility for the Shaffer children was to care for

"Wahoo" the goat, 1935

"Wahoo," the family goat. A backyard pen was built for their lively pet and they discovered quickly that nothing was sacred. The fence had to be strong, because Wahoo's appetite was never ending. If let loose, he would eat every vegetable, herb and cut flower in their yard and the neighbors' yards, including Ethel's prized rose bush.

Although his disorderly conduct seemed to be a problem, Wahoo was a wonderful companion for the children. Their grandfather built a cart with wheels that were salvaged from chairs at the Bloomsburg hospital. Daily, the goat was allowed to pull the children around the yard, stopping at designated places to eat weeds and brush.

His contributions to the compost pile created good tilth for the garden, and he would stay with the family for years to come.

As the winter season brought snow, ice and cold, Ethel found alternate ways to help contribute financially. After gathering fresh evergreen boughs, holly, blue spruce and German statice, she made blankets of the fresh greens to cover graves. Decorated with pine cones and an abundant red bow, the blankets were handmade with care. Included on each one was a "Christmas in Heaven" inscription. With the leftover greens, fresh wreaths were made, a traditional festive Christmas symbol. These quickly sold as they evoked memories of family gatherings past.

ETHEL'S ROOTBEER / SASSAFRAS SODA

Ingredients:
6 cups water
3 ounces sassafras roots
1 ounce dandelion root
¼ cup molasses
1 clove
1 star anise
1 teaspoon coriander seeds
2 drops wintergreen extract
6 cups sugar

Chop both types of roots into 1/2 inch pieces or smaller.
Add the roots to a heavy pan along with clove, anise, and coriander.
Add water, cover pan and bring to a boil. Simmer for 15 minutes.
Add molasses, and simmer 5 more minutes.
Turn off the stove and add extract. Put cover back on.
After cooling, strain through cheesecloth.
Return to pan and add sugar. Stir well. Simmer for 5 minutes, uncovered.
Store in mason jars and seal. Will stay good in icebox for up to a year.

Serve a tablespoon or two with
a pint of carbonated water.

~ 5 ~

Fun and Friends
The Single Years

To her classmates, Catherine Shaffer was described as filled with energy and life. Her friends loved her sassy personality and well-developed sense of humor – attributes which made lasting friendships long after graduation.

Her keen interest in learning coupled with strong leadership and community service involvement awarded her an invitation to speak at the Bloomsburg High School Commencement.

It was 1941 and as World War II continued to rage in Europe and the Pacific, many men were called upon to fight for their country. In an auditorium filled with red and white, Catherine addressed the graduating Panthers and the entire school community on world conditions.

A topic that would be boring to some captured the interest of the audience. Looking out into a sea of graduating caps, this

Father And Daughter Are Enrolled In Defense Courses

Orval Shaffer, of town, and his daughter Miss Katherine are among those who are enrolled in the defense courses being offered by the Pennsylvania State College at the local Teachers College.

Catherine and her father, 1942

spirited and lively young woman focused on the important
contributions that women were making on the home front.
While men were away, it was the women who took on factory
jobs and were responsible for the production and supplies that
the troops needed.

Her message rang loud and clear that in a historically
male-dominated workplace, trades like welding and engine
repair were being done well by women. During wartime and
after, the fruits of their labor would need to be remembered,
not only for their efforts, but for equal pay as well.

To contribute to the war efforts, Catherine volunteered
as an air warden. Wearing helmets and arm bands, together
with her father, they patrolled the neighborhood after dark.
Laws required that all windows and doors were covered with
government material preventing the slightest glow of light.

"Blackout Regulations" were strictly enforced as even the slightest glimmer of light could aid enemy aircraft. (Picture of Catherine & her father attending class)

Although these regulations disrupted many activities, people regarded this as a patriotic duty and did their part to ensure safety on the home front.

After completing this academic milestone and to save for college, Catherine eagerly accepted a position with the Pennsylvania Department of Forest and Water. With a real love for nature and wildlife, she was excited to start her job, working 8-4.

On her first day, Catherine chose a simple knee length skirt, back seam thigh high stockings and a tailored blouse with square shoulder pads. She passed over typical high heels for a comfortable low-heeled shoe in anticipation of spending time on her feet. Her shoulder length dark brown hair was styled with soft curls and parted on the side.

Her beautiful smile and positive perspective created a climate that put everyone at ease, including the forest rangers. The rangers worked diligently to protect the state land and natural resources. In addition, hikers and campers were instructed to respect the woodlands as trails were maintained, water supplies were improved and forest fires were fought. The busy office staff was responsible for several other tasks. Many parks were being developed and licenses were required on all boats using the

Catherine, 1941

23

Jackie, 1942

waterways. As a secretary for the district forester, Catherine's job kept her moving. From down the hall one could hear the keystroke sounds and the carriage return bell as she cranked out documents daily. She loved typing on her new glossy black typewriter. The Smith-Corona was a real workhorse and made her job much more efficient.

On weekends, Catherine and her sister Jackie welcomed the chance to go camping. It was a great escape from the work week and also an excellent way to save money. Jackie had developed a real love for oil painting and it was here that she found her artistic talents were best expressed. The experience itself was worth much more to her than the finished piece and often the colors and strokes conveyed a message that might have been difficult to express in words.

"I experience a period of frightening clarity and in these moments when nature is so beautiful I am no longer sure of myself and the paintings appear as in a dream."

~ Vincent van Gogh

There was nothing quite like spending time in the great outdoors under nature's hood with people they enjoyed. Long-time friends, Betty Martz and Mary Lou Fenstemacher had an open invitation to join them.

The weekend kicked off with lots of laughter and warm chatter. Still, they appreciated the retreat; nature's silence and the untouched state of the land left them yearning to return. By day, the group packed a lunch and hit the hiking trails at World's End State Park. They made a track up the mountain to the lookout fire tower. There they took in the views of the Endless mountains and observed the unforgettable scenery.

Catherine's co-worker and forest ranger, Clair McCarty, knew of her love for the great outdoors. Often, he'd loan her his Indian Motorcycle to enjoy on the weekends. Equipped with a sidecar, the light-weight bike toured World's End Park while the riders took in the beautiful scenery.

After miles of walking, the group returned to the campsite famished and devoured hot dogs on a stick cooked over the campfire, while Mary Lou and Betty prepared soup. The combination of lentils, carrots, garlic, onions and a dash of salt and pepper offered up a delicious aroma that made the campsite smell wonderful. As the campfire died down and the day came to an end, the girls savored a rich cup of coffee and some traditional tasty s'mores. With a full weekend of activity and plenty of fresh air they were relaxed, rested and ready to return to work on Monday.

Catherine, 1942

Catherine left the campgrounds in plenty of time for her Sunday school class. Attending "Sabbath School" as a child, she knew the importance of building positive friendships and having fun. It was one of the most consistent programs in her church and she enjoyed teaching religion in an educational setting.

Her favorite groups were the small, wiggly five and six-year olds. Catherine helped them discover Biblical truths. Telling a flannel board story was a magical way to engage the children and brought the story alive. In addition, coloring pictures, making crafts and singing songs were all part of the hour that passed by quickly. Warmth and love flowed in her classroom as Catherine truly cared about each child and knew their names and their needs. The students learned and were challenged but how much more did life have in store for Catherine? As a Christian role model, she would continue to support, influence and inspire the faith of children for many years to come.

~ 6 ~

College and Friendships

When it came time to attend college, the very Reverend Malcolm Hunsicker helped guide her major and career decisions. After discussing skills, interests and values, his encouragement was to channel Catherine's love for children and passion by teaching. This led her to the Philadelphia Institute where she would receive her degree in Christian Education.

It was a small campus and the school offered an outstanding balance of religious life and liberal arts academics. The simple, brick, ivy-covered buildings with historical architecture and stained glass offered a pretty, collegiate setting. Footpaths between buildings made it easy to get to and from the dorm, library, classrooms and dining hall.

Receiving a work scholarship from the institute was a great financial help to Catherine. By day she balanced her classes with light housekeeping and prep work in the kitchen. At night, she would study with roommates, Grace Lewis and Gladys Dudley.

left to right: Dud, Catherine and Grace, 1945

Gladys, born and raised in Culpeper, Virginia was a true southern belle. Along with good manners and southern charm, her honey sweet personality and warm smile put everyone at ease.

Grace, referred to by her friends as "Amazing Grace" arrived in Philadelphia from the all-American city of Ansonia, Connecticut. With so many similar interests, she and Catherine hit it off instantaneously.

Their special place to study was at the school library. Over a hundred years old, the library was a warm and cozy retreat after a long day in the classrooms. The soft, leather library chairs were a comfortable place to start. With tufted backs and arms supported by balusters, the seats were raised on turned legs and seemed to fit any frame like a glove. Students migrated to the oak card catalog cases, and using the brass pulls, opened the drawers to research reading material. Individually listed on each card was every book registered in the library and a location to find it.

Head Librarian Helen Maderes made sure the library was well-stocked and well-staffed. In addition to helping students with their needs, the robust mahogany study desks were waxed and polished daily by the workers. They showed a beautiful grain of color and the matching wood chairs with slatted backs kept the "too relaxed" students alert and encouraged the continuation of their studies. The heavy brass lamps operated with a pull chain and were aged and dark. They had a beautiful cream and orange color that ran throughout the marble base, a timeless look providing much needed light.

On cold winter nights, the faint whistling sounds of the steam radiators could be heard as they worked overtime to provide warmth. Large oriental rugs covered the majority of the worn wood floors and were the soul of the main rooms. Resilient and made with a fine weave, the classic, ornate floral pattern kept the noise levels to a minimum and provided additional warmth and comfort.

Grace, Gladys and Catherine spent hours here studying and developing life-long friendships that would continue for many years, long after their 1946 graduation.

The years after college graduation passed surprisingly quickly. Although time flew by, the memories she collected at school with her friends were never replaced, only new ones made.

Catherine kept in touch with Gladys and Grace through letters and phone calls. They discussed all the things that close friends

Catherine, 1946

would share and might even disclose in a diary. Mostly work and hobbies, but recently relationships were a popular topic. At the age of 26, Catherine seriously started to think about meeting a happily ever after person that she could fall in love with for a lifetime. As she cherished working with children, she thought of what it would be like to have her own family.

College was complete and she was enjoying her occupation. Despite many interests, friends and family, she was missing someone special and wanted to start dating. Loving and trustworthy were two qualities in a man that mattered to her as well as generous, successful and funny. Someone who would make her heart beat just a little bit faster. Someone whose voice put a smile on her face and she looked forward to hearing. But just where was this special man?

Mrs. Franke

*I*t was 1949 and the country was seeing a major movement of population from rural areas to cities. It seemed like small town America was being left behind by the Christian community. Rural missionaries like Catherine were needed and in high demand. Part of their work involved reopening and strengthening churches and reaching out to this overlooked part of American society.

Catherine had been assigned to Westfield, Pennsylvania. It was the perfect place as the town was two hours away from Bloomsburg. Her mother had developed heart problems and she could easily return home more frequently for visits. Westfield had grown on her since graduation and she felt like it was her second home.

Her salary as a rural missionary paid $250 monthly. To keep expenses to a minimum, she rented a room right after graduation from an elderly lady named Mrs. Franke, who became a dear friend.

Mrs. Franke resided on Elm Street, which was composed of a charming blend of beautifully preserved row houses and stately executive homes. The neighborhood offered not only timeless charm but an atmosphere of comfort and a sense of place. There was a wonderful canopy of mature trees that lined the inviting street and with walkable sidewalks it was a true community where neighbors knew and looked out for each other.

Mrs. Franke provided spacious, comfortable and clean short-term accommodations, yet after four years, she was in no hurry to have Catherine leave and vice versa.

As a tenant, her private entrance faced a garden atrium. The bright and roomy bedroom included a Birdseye maple set. It was in pristine condition and both dressers had carved, beveled mirrors. There was plenty of room for her clothes and the one chest included a hat box at the top. The comfortable bed displayed a double wedding quilt. The hand-pieced work of art showcased a cheerful palette of pastel colors and beautifully brightened the bedroom. The hardwood floors were polished and located next to the large window was a big walk in closet for additional storage. Her quarters were at the other end of the house, which offered privacy and her own bathroom.

In addition to the weekly $25 room and board fee, Catherine drove Mrs. Franke on errands in her 1946 Chevy. The car was well cared for and had its own home in the attached garage. She also did some light housekeeping and helped prepare a few meals every week.

Mondays were wash day, and the new Maytag wringer washer was a delight to use. The whites were washed first, followed by lights and then darks last. It was an efficient way to clean clothes, save time and conserve water and detergent. On fine weather days, the wash was pegged to the backyard clothesline. If Monday's forecast called for rain, the laundry was placed on drying racks inside.

Together they would go
through Mrs. Franke's cook-
books and select some easy-to-
make comfort meals. Roasted
chicken, potato salad and lemon
meringue pie were some of the
many favorites. The two warmed
to each other quickly and their
friendship over the years made
parting difficult when it was
time for Catherine to leave. For
Mrs. Franke, her life was rekin-
dled with the young woman's
vibrancy and for Catherine, the
knowledge and wisdom that the
elderly woman offered brought
rich, meaningful conversation
for her and provided a wealth of
knowledge that would be useful
to Catherine for years to come.

*Mrs. Franke and her husband
William, 1947*

They enjoyed spending time in the kitchen. Mrs. Franke
loved sharing her cooking skills and family recipes with Catherine. Side by side, one of their favorite autumn dishes was
pot roast. Every Tuesday morning a delivery of fresh chuck
roast, carefully selected by the butcher, arrived at the back
door wrapped in brown paper and string. Mrs. Franke always
ordered enough meat to include a beef stroganoff dish to eat
later in the week. They both made perfectly warm meals on
cool fall evenings.

After work, Catherine would return home to find Mrs.
Franke at the stove with the initial preparations started.
The smell of onions browning in olive oil was a welcome
retreat after a long day of work. The elderly lady wore
an apron that was also used for household chores. It was

obvious that the apron had aged gracefully over time. The smock had a pattern of strawberry fields and bright red checked gingham. Deep pockets adorned the front and were accented with red rick rack. Catherine often wondered just how many meals Mrs. Franke had prepared with care while wearing this cover.

The large cast iron skillet had been in the family for generations and held heat well. It seemed to bring out the taste of every ingredient.

Catherine wasn't sure if it was the generous use of salt and ground pepper, the fresh thyme and rosemary or the patience taken to create this well thought out dish that made it so delicious. The fork-tender, flavorful meat, homemade mashed potatoes, garden fresh carrots along with the gravy made from pan drippings created a melt-in-your-mouth meal to be savored.

After the last dish was washed and dried, the ladies retreated to the front parlor for conversation and to listen to a favorite radio show. It was the first room in the home located off the foyer. Guests were invited in and for years it was opened to the family for special use on Sundays.

Recently, Catherine had encouraged her friend to consider enjoying the beautiful space more frequently as she had taken great pride in decorating the parlor. To assure the guests would feel welcomed and comfortable, she chose a redwood sofa that faced the fireplace, accompanied by two soft easy chairs. The fanciful wallpaper was attractive, yet blended nicely with the woodwork and quiet color carpet. The center table accommodated three to four people and could easily be used for Parcheesi or reading.

Brass lamps with gold leaf finish and the pleated shades gave a warm, ambient feel throughout the room. Artistic thought went into the careful selection of oil paintings and plentiful portraits of relatives were arranged as a reminder of those present and loved ones who had gone on.

A new Philco receiver sat proudly in the corner of the room and the art deco look fit the parlor surroundings beautifully. This was the center of entertainment and helped pass the time on many evenings. As they were settling in to hear "Amos and Andy," Mrs. Franke recalled an earlier event that happened that day. The normal delivery of mail was through a slot in the front door, yet at two o'clock, the Westminster melody of the doorbell alerted the homeowner of a visitor. Mr. Moore stood outside the front entrance. Dressed in his gray bell crown cap and Eisenhower jacket, he had spotted a letter posted to Catherine. Concerned it might be of urgency, he wanted to make sure she received the post promptly. After placing a log on the fire, Mrs. Franke retrieved the letter and gave it to Catherine.

~ 8 ~

Bomboy's Market

$\mathcal{A}$ s the years passed and the children grew older, Catherine's parents' once-lively home that was filled with a flurry of activity transitioned into an empty nest. The absence of people was replaced with family pictures that abounded throughout the home. For a parent, this stillness could be a heart-rending change and a natural sense of loss, especially for a woman like Ethel whose identity was defined by her children.

After completing school, Jackie and Nadine were married and lived in nearby towns. Orval Jr. finished his service in the army and also was wed. For Catherine, she continued to enjoy her work as a rural missionary in Westfield. This left Richard at home, nearing high school graduation.

Ethel now had the opportunity to expand her life with new hobbies and friendships, and she did! With less laundry, fewer groceries and more time, she no longer had the day-to-day constraints of a full house. After watching her children mature and function as adults, she looked forward to some well-deserved time for herself and for Orval. She knew her

The Shaffer family, 1941

job as a mother was not over once they left home, it was simply different – she would now cultivate friendships with her grown children.

Now that they had more discretionary income, this afforded Ethel and Orval the opportunity to travel to Westfield to visit their daughter. Packed and ready to go on the first Friday of every month, the 1948 Hudson had a powerful engine for its time and guaranteed the two hour trip to be enjoyable. It was a smooth ride, including a considerably large interior with soft, velvet-like seats. Hudsons had an excellent design for mid- to upper range cars, including the bulging trunk lid capable of holding more than average packages. The washed and waxed black exterior showcased the silver trim with side lighting that would make heads turn.

Before leaving town, they always made a stop at Bomboy's Market on East Street and 7th. Howard and Hattie Bomboy were the proud owners of a store that provided a variety of groceries and a sense of community. Every customer who walked through the door was greeted and called by name. They were also good friends of the Shaffers. Their daughter Getha, along with Jackie and Catherine, worked in the market after school, weighing and bagging flour, sugar, rice and beans and keeping the store neat and clean. The shelves were lined with linen and stocked with canned goods. The old-fashioned cooler held a variety of cheeses, soda pop and ice cream. People travelled far and wide for Howard's Lebanon Bologna. A Pennsylvania Dutch meat, Lebanon Bologna combined a tangy palette of spices and beef that cured in a wooden smokehouse for days. Served on a roll with zesty mustard, along with a barrel-cured pickle, it was a great treat on any day.

On this Friday, Hattie and Howard were looking forward to the Shaffers stopping by the market, because Elizabeth Corse, a long-time friend, was visiting from Patterson, New Jersey. Hattie was eager to introduce these families. The Bomboys savored many years of friendship, socializing at the Corse's waterfront cottage on Cranberry Lake. While the youngsters played as a group, enjoying backyard sports and lake activities, the adults visited and got to know each other well. Establishing lifelong friends seemed like something everyone did and it was normal in those days. Even the children developed friendships that would last well into their adult lives.

Hattie was very fond of Elizabeth's son, Kenneth. He was a fine young man, educated and employed as a tool designer working in Patterson. Kenneth had all the qualities that would make an outstanding husband and father. However, he was lacking a romantic partner. Hattie was also very partial to the Shaffer's eldest daughter, Catherine.

Although Catherine kept busy with her work and had an active life, she too was missing that one important component, a lifelong companion. Today might be the perfect time for the families to get acquainted followed by an arrangement for Catherine and Kenneth to meet.

At the back of the market was a lovely kitchenette where the afternoon tea would take place. Before the table was laid, a Victoria Sponge cake had been baked with readiness that morning. Named after Queen Victoria, the cake consisted of raspberry jam and whipped double cream sandwiched between two sponge cakes and dusted with caster sugar.

Soft pale pink linen covered the round oak table with matching napkins. Hattie chose her bone china tea set to impress the guests. Made and imported from England, the china appeared strong, yet was delicate and accompanied by English grace and elegance. The set featured gold edging and a soft pink rose décor. Stately cups were designed to be held by pinching the handle with the thumb and index finger.

The mid-afternoon tea consisted of a hint of Earl Grey and Jasmine. Each cup would be a mystery as the flavors were noted at different times. One could almost feel the soft floral notes of jasmine while getting the satisfaction of bergamot orange, a fragrant citrus fruit found in Earl Grey. The loose tea was brewed in the teapot and served with milk and sugar. Hattie felt the sugar and caffeine might help prevent afternoon doldrums.

Howard looked forward to a visit with Orval. He had just completed a storefront bench and had it proudly sitting outside. He used cypress wood to build the bench as it was a perfect choice for a natural preservative. Cypress repelled rain, snow, and sun and over time would weather to a handsome gray. Howard was pleased with the outcome as it would last for decades, standing the test of time and nature. To him, there was nothing like a bench to inspire the feeling of serenity.

As the nation recovered from the Great Depression, the streets in Bloomsburg were a place where people came together and entrepreneurial spirit flourished. Packards, Studebakers, Pontiacs and other post-war cars were parked out in front of the store while American flags lined the streets. A storefront bench was the perfect place to chat, smoke a rich cigar and visit with the town residents as they went about their daily lives.

~ *9* ~

The Arrangement

"Pleasure has no relish unless we share it."

~ Virginia Wolfe

*I*n what could have been a highly charged emotional situation, the afternoon tea turned out to be successful. Hattie knew if Ethel and Elizabeth developed a friendship without being forced, it would be beneficial to everyone.

Conversation flowed effortlessly from one topic to the next. All three ladies discovered common books they had read and enjoyed. "A Diary of a Young Girl" and "A Tree Grows in Brooklyn" were unexpected mutual delights and they all found a safe place to exchange their ideas on the stories.

Favorite, once-loved hobbies from their youth had returned. With more free time on their hands, embroidery was a common "thread." Everything from linen, frames, needles, scissors, and hoops were discussed. Ethel enthusiastically shared her new form of recreation: painting. It was therapeutic and fulfilling for her, and inspiring and fascinating just listening to the description of her garden sketches.

They chose to engage in these interests – they didn't have to. The post–depression, post–war times afforded these leisurely activities and brought great balance into their lives.

When Hattie brought up the subject of Kenneth and Catherine, both ladies were in unanimous agreement that the couple should meet. Conversation was comfortable and smooth and everyone was excited about the potential courtship.

Upon completion of their dining experience, the napkins were folded with a crease and placed to the left side of the place setting, indicating to the host that they wished to be invited back.

In just one short afternoon, both families found much in common, including two long time married couples who wanted so much happiness for their children.

Elizabeth recognized that Catherine was smart, attractive and accomplished. Her introduction to Kenneth could be a perfect match and Elizabeth wanted to fully capitalize on this good fortune. She couldn't wait to return to New Jersey and share the positive news with the family and suggest that Kenneth make a very important call as soon as possible.

~ *10* ~

A Special Letter and Phone Call

The letter was postmarked November 4th, 1949 from Patterson, New Jersey. While reaching for the letter opener, Catherine was trying to recall any acquaintances that she knew from the Garden state. After loosening the crease with the sharp writing companion, Catherine carefully removed the letter from the envelope, glancing at the smart, moleskin paper. The stationary was simple, yet classic in design and the initials "KJC" adorned the top of the paper.

The letter was light and positive as the writer explained his mother's recent visit to Bloomsburg included tea with Hattie Bomboy and Ethel Shaffer. While the ladies had discussed many topics, the conversation continued to circle back to one subject. In unanimous agreement, they all felt Kenneth and Catherine should meet.

The handwriting was neat and precise, and it looked like the words glided across the paper, naturally and effortlessly forming crisp and fine lines, a hint that the writer was familiar with the use of a fountain pen.

Kenneth explained his reason for writing: that he would be in Bloomsburg for business on the weekend of November 18th. Apologizing for short notice, he asked "would you be interested in meeting?" His words were complimentary and sincere. As Hattie had provided him with Catherine's information, he said he would attempt to reach her by phone on November 10th at seven o'clock in the evening.

Although the communication was short, it served its purpose: to secure Catherine's respect and consideration and influence their future. She lit up as she read the words over again. The paper that had once been in his hands was now in hers and she was happy. She looked forward to the call in just a few brief days.

Between a busy work week, multiple errands and cleaning for Mrs. Franke, Catherine found the time breezing by. Thursday arrived and as she traveled home from work, her mind once again drifted to the seven o'clock call with Kenneth. Nervous yet excited, she looked forward to hearing his voice and meeting him for the "first time" by phone. It made her feel special.

The 1940s was a time of innovation and those with telephones had this communication luxury. The Western Electric had a prominent place on the entryway table, known as "the gossip bench." It was a time when people could pay attention to a conversation without interruptions or multi-tasking. Leaning back in the rich upholstery was relaxing and the thick padded armrests offered added comfort. The built-in side table for the phone was convenient, with a drawer below that held the phone book, writing paper and pens.

Two short ring tones were assigned to the Franke household alerting them to incoming calls. The only downside to this form of communication was a shared phone line with neighbors. "Party lines" in those days prevented people from total privacy, allowing others to potentially eavesdrop on personal conversations.

After a quick bowl of Spanish rice, she glanced at the hall clock. It was 6:55pm. Her heart raced with anticipation as she knew he would be dialing in a few short minutes.

The call came at 7:00 sharp. Catherine listened carefully, smiling naturally as the deep voice on the other end greeted her warmly. She was expecting a North Jersey accent yet his pronunciations were more like her friends and family from Philadelphia.

Not every second was taken with conversation, yet they were able to avoid awkward silences. Her voice "smiled" and they laughed at how their families felt they should meet. Catherine's quick wit brought on a hearty laugh from Ken as she told him her only reason for meeting him was her Father. Since the Bomboys were close family friends, he had insisted that Catherine was to follow through with the arrangement.

Kenneth was traveling through Bloomsburg on business, staying at the Magee Hotel for the weekend and said he would like to see her while he was there. After a short volley back and forth, the two wrapped things up in a polite way, agreeing to meet on Saturday at her family home. In a few days, their next encounter would be face-to-face.

Heading Home

The Shaffer household would be bustling with people for the autumn weekend. Orval Jr. and Richard had already made plans to be home with the family. While the brothers made repairs on the homestead, their wives, Eileen and Gerry, enjoyed getting to know their newly extended family and learning from Ethel how to can and preserve all the fall garden goodies. Harvest preparations helped stretch the budget and kept them in delicious vegetables through the winter. Without modern distractions, families enjoyed spending time together as they did on this day, in the simple act of creating provisions for the barren months ahead.

Catherine had warned her brothers in advance to be on their best behavior because company was coming. She hoped her request would not fall on deaf ears, as the two siblings tended to be quite the tease. She took comfort in knowing her father would be present. A certain glance from him would cease any mischief from her brothers. By the parental example that was set over the years, Orval and Ethel had earned well-deserved respect.

Catherine pulled into the Texaco and was greeted by the station owner, Mr. Johnston. Gas had climbed up to 18 cents per gallon but she didn't mind. The excellent service she received was well worth the price. While the tank was filled, the middle-aged man attended to checking the water and oil, washed the windows and put air in the tires, all routine tasks in those days. Mr. Johnston enjoyed working on Catherine's car and considered it a gem.

With a three-speed manual transmission, the 1946 Chevy was one of the first American civilian cars and a great seller in the immediate post war period. Catherine spared no expense with this investment. The grey cloth seats and an AM radio made the interior special while the outside boasted lots of chrome in the fenders, skirts and bumpers. She spent a little extra for the rich, color-matching full windshield and sun visor and it looked attractive in the deep maroon color.

The trip to Bloomsburg seemed faster than usual. Her mind was preoccupied, thoughts bouncing between last night's call and the sadness of her mother's declining health. She was thankful to live in close driving distance. Pulling into the driveway, she parking next to the family Hudson and spotted a bonfire outback. Orval was tending to the fire while Pappy stirred a big iron pot of apple butter. It continued to boil until thick while the aroma of sweet apples brought back many fond memories.

She grabbed her bag out of the trunk and ran up the front porch stairs. It was so good to be home.

The slam of the wooden screen door alerted the family that the eldest daughter had arrived. She made her way to the central hub of the house, where the busy comings and goings took place. There Catherine found her Mom, Granny, Eileen and Gerry busy paring and coring winesaps for the apple butter.

A simmering stock pot of vegetable soup was kept warm on the stove for the weary traveler. The smell of warm apple pie and the crusty homemade bread just taken out of the oven reminded her of the many reasons she was glad to be home on this chilly fall night.

She filled her bowl with steaming hot soup and pulled a chair up to join the ladies at the table. Winter vegetable soup was one of Catherine's favorites, hearty and full of fresh produce. She dipped the soup spoon into the bowl and the warm broth along with honey wheat bread satisfied her appetite. A cup of chamomile tea provided her with much needed relaxation to calm her nerves. The large oak table had been in the center of the kitchen for as long as she could remember. Her Pappy had built the solid over-sized table along with the chairs. Besides being used for family meals, the table provided a place to can vegetables, make jams and chutney, pack pickles and bottle herbs for storage.

The warmth in the kitchen was not only coming from the stove but from each face that brightened the room. Catherine felt cozy, warm and wonderful. Laughing and chatting, the mutual enjoyment of each other's company was never taken for granted.

Within minutes it was clear that news of the couple meeting on Saturday had spread like wildfire. The family was excited and full of questions. Ethel Shaffer and Hattie Bomboy had done their part in getting the word out. Catherine shuddered to think what the morning paper would bring.

While Eileen and Gerry cleaned up the kitchen, Catherine retreated to the living room to spend time with her mother. Concerned for her mom, they visited for a while. It was clear that her mother's health was deteriorating and Catherine could sense she was sad and frustrated with her diminished capacities. More than ever she would continue to maintain a good relationship with her parents.

After helping her get settled for the night, Catherine looked at her watch. Tomorrow would be a busy day. She took her suitcase and made her way to the guest room for the night.

~ *12* ~

*A Visitor Arrives
at the Hotel Magee*

At the peak of the hotel era, The Hotel Magee, located on West Main Street was one of the most luxurious and sought after hotels in the area. As Kenneth pulled up, he could see several bellmen helping guests with their luggage while the valet personnel assisted with parking automobiles. Instructed to make a first good impression, the front house staff were dressed in sharp uniform attire and were friendly and courteous.

The evening bellmen took their jobs seriously making sure every guest that came and went was greeted warmly. There was something to be said for uniformity in those days. Buttoned panel front burgundy jackets with coordinating black pants were pressed and perfect. The pillbox hats were made fit to size and the shoes were polished to perfection.

Hotel Magee, 1940

Kenneth checked into a suite on the third floor and was pleasantly surprised by how spacious it was. Recent renovations consisted of beautiful furnishings and a modern bathroom. He was fortunate to get such a nice room. The hotel was sold out with people traveling out of their way to stay at the Magee.

Declining room service, he chose to eat in the dining room as a "dress rehearsal" and enjoyed a rack of lamb. Returning to his room, he listened to a radio show and then turned in for a restful night.

As he laid in bed, he thought of Catherine. Ken looked forward to their meeting tomorrow. He couldn't wait to see her and get to know her better. With heavy eyes, he drifted off to sleep keeping those thoughts in mind.

Kenneth woke up the next morning refreshed from a good night's sleep. As he opened the drapes to welcome the morning sun, thoughts drifted back to Catherine. After checking phone messages with the hotel operator he headed down to the gym.

One of the hotel amenities was an exercise room and he took full advantage of the pulley machine, something he'd gotten into the habit of doing back home. Surprised to find no one there, he started the day with a good sweat.

Upon returning to his room, he took a hot shower and headed to the dining room for breakfast. There was something about morning exercise that brought on a ravenous appetite. The buttermilk pancakes, with a side of eggs over easy and maple bacon sounded scrumptious. While waiting for his food, he sipped a tall glass of juice and opened the paper. The orange juice was freshly squeezed and delicious.

After finishing the last bite of breakfast, Kenneth headed upstairs to get ready for the day. Opening the closet, he chose a collared shirt and trousers. He preferred to avoid formality, yet he wanted to show respect for her, knowing how much first impressions matter. It was too late into the fall season to be considered an Indian summer, yet it was unseasonably warm for that time of year. Before leaving he took a sweater as they would be spending most of the day outside. Today's weather would be a great opportunity to soak in the sun as winter was fast approaching.

After the car was brought up, he made one quick stop at the Straddling greenhouses to pick up an order of flowers. After that he would be on his way to meet Catherine.

~ *13* ~

An Autumn First Date

*I*t was the first nip in the air on a cool November morning. The sky was sea blue with bright sunshine. What a perfect day to spend at Arbutus Park, Catherine thought.

She stood at the mirror to take one last look. She felt more excited than nervous. Their phone conversation had left her intrigued and she was happy that the call had broken the ice for today's visit with Kenneth.

The navy polka dot skirt she chose was stylish and very feminine and it paired beautifully with a weightless crepe blouse. She took her favorite cardigan from the suitcase and put it on. The super soft sweater would keep her warm today. Sliding on a pair of navy flats completed the look and the shoes were comfortable for walking.

Her makeup was fresh and natural, the way she liked it and she selected a shade that was close to her normal lip color. After a light spritz of "Miss Dior" she ran downstairs to answer the bell.

Standing at the door was a sharply dressed man with an attractive physique. His warm smile put Catherine at ease almost instantaneously. "It's so good to meet you, Catherine," he said tenderly, grasping her hand. "Here, these are for you," as he placed the autumn bouquet in her arms.

Elegantly arranged, the flowers consisted of yellow chrysanthemums, roses and lilies. Tucked in the bouquet were orange gerbera miniatures and oak leaves, all tied with a yellow satin ribbon. Catherine recognized the work of art to be one of Mr. Straddling's creations. "Thank you, Kenneth, they're beautiful!" "Please, call me Ken." "Alright then, Ken it is!"

After some family introductions the two headed outside to get acquainted on the front porch. This was Catherine's favorite place to spend time when she got home. In those days, porches told a story about life back then. The extension of living space brought neighbors and community together. Even though folks were busy, it was here that they found tranquility and created memories. The porch was a place to pause, especially on harried days, lighten the pace and savor the present moment.

The Shaffer's porch was designed to welcome and provide relaxation. Lined with rockers and a big porch swing, it was an open invitation for folks to drop by for a visit and sit a spell. Whether it was a spring day, a hot summer evening or an autumn afternoon, it offered a refreshing escape.

Catherine only knew this too well as they drifted back and forth on the swing. The conversation flowed and was mixed with humor and enjoyable chatter.

Occasionally he found himself drifting from a topic to glance at her attractive smile that flashed his way. The expression in her face was sincere and genuine, and the combination of sparkle in her eyes and the full soft lips made him happy. He enjoyed watching her talk as the upper lip had a gentle curve that peaked like a cupid's bow.

He was relaxed and drawn to her and knew immediately that she was certainly worth getting to know.

"We shall never know all the good
that a simple smile can do."

~ Mother Teresa

Getting close to lunchtime, they took a picnic basket and headed to Arbutus Park. It was a brisk fall day, a perfect time for a walk in the park. The air was cooler, but the sun beamed down beautifully, keeping them warm. The couple remarked about the changing colors of the foliage: a beautiful palate of bright yellows, deep reds, mahogany browns and lively orange, many already fallen, covering the ground. Catherine collected a variety of leaves for her mother to enjoy.

As they walked along the path it felt good to take in the clean, crisp air. Up ahead, they found a perfect place to dine. While Ken spread out the blanket, Catherine unpacked the lunch. She found much in him that she was drawn to. He appeared socially at ease and it was obvious that he was genuinely interested in her. From a physical perspective, she noticed his broad shoulders and narrow hips. His stylish watch and sleeves rolled up on a classic shirt indicated his personality and style, and signaled his close attention to detail. What impressed her most was his confident not cocky nature... sensitive yet strong characteristics. She felt safe around him and was enjoying their time together. It was time well spent.

They enjoyed a lunch of ham salad sandwiches, ice-box cookies, fruit and bottled root beer. It was easy to be relaxed while staring at nature's beauty and listening to the birds singing. The weather could not have been better for their first date.

On the way home, Ken reached out with a tender touch and took her hand. His fondness and respect for Catherine made her feel special and she was happy. This delicate stepping stone turned out to be comfortable and romantic. After returning Catherine to her parent's home, he headed back to the hotel to finish some business while Catherine visited relatives for the afternoon.

Since they resided relatively far apart, they both agreed to make the most of the weekend. Ken made dinner reservations that evening at the Magee Hotel and arranged to pick up Catherine at seven o'clock.

The afternoon had flown and by six thirty she had finished dressing. Night had closed in and the air was chilled. Her tweed pencil skirt and cashmere sweater would keep her warm. She added a few striking accessories, then reached for her black woolen coat and clutch bag. He was right on time.

The hotel was busy and Ken was relieved that he had made a reservation. As they walked through the dining room it was interesting to note the menu choices that guests had selected. Food at the Magee was five star in both presentation and taste.

The restaurant was stunning. Tables were adorned with crisp linens and vases filled with fresh flowers. They were seated close to a large window overlooking the illuminated fountains and gardens. Catherine loved his attention to detail, as he opened the doors and pulled out the chairs for her. Working in the Department of Forestry, the majority of employees were men. She got along well with them and the co-workers appreciated Catherine, but they lacked polish when it came to manners. These extra touches were long overdue and a welcome change to the normal work week.

Ken's compliments made her blush, yet she enjoyed them. The two laughed while glancing at the menu, noting some interesting contrasts in food preferences, but they also found some common ground.

Catherine ordered first, selecting the chicken a la king with biscuit and curried carrots. Ken chose a pork chop with glazed sweet potatoes and herb and apple compote. "Glory Buns," a spiced bread, were delivered to the table and while waiting for the meal the pair enjoyed Bellini cocktails. It was a delightful night and she noticed how he made eye contact while talking and listening to her. Her response was reciprocated when she gazed into his brown eyes. It was as if the entire room was empty except for the two of them.

Soon the meal was brought out and within minutes both agreed that it was delicious and worth waiting for. A complimentary side dish of vegetables was served as well. These came from the "Victory Gardens," which was a way to help support local farmers who planted vegetables after the war.

Dinner ended with fresh perked coffee and rich and spicy pumpkin pie, served warm with whipped cream.

Hand-in-hand, the couple left the hotel for a post dessert stroll. Stars filled the evening sky and the night wind was cool. Yet gentle. It was a night that Ken wished would never end. He felt like he had finally found someone whom he could envision having as a girlfriend and possibly more. He wanted to get to know her better. He was concerned about the distance because of his obligations at work. He decided he would bear the burden of travel, as he didn't want to put any more responsibility on Catherine, with her mom's health issues weighing on her. She also was coming quite a few miles from Westfield.

She pulled her scarf close to her neck and felt the breeze send a chill though her coat. He must have sensed her shivering as he put his arm around her shoulder. Thoughts were racing through her head, mostly good things, yet Catherine was concerned. Was the timing right? How would she care for her Mom? Could she keep up with her work in Westfield and help with Mrs. Franke, who was getting older? There was so much to think about but one thing was certain, she hadn't been this happy in a very long time.

As he walked her to the door and bid her good night, they embraced while he gave her a warm, lingering kiss. The signals were very clear and they agreed to keep in touch through letters and calls, knowing they would see each other again in just a few short weeks.

*Ken's 1936 Oldsmobile. The car he
courted Catherine in.*

~ *14* ~

A Holiday Courtship

*W*ith great anticipation, the couple looked forward to receiving each other's letters. Both physically alone, but mentally with each other, the words helped them paint a more profound and sincere picture of themselves.

Their affection grew and with ease the true thoughts they shared became more natural in writing. There was something magical in the written words that made them laugh, and by re-reading the notes and sharing photographs, they came to life, bringing the two closer together.

His words and expressions made her blush, yet gave her great pleasure. There was a natural intimacy. And her letters to him captured his heart. In a short time they had fallen closer in love, yearning for their next encounter when they could be together again.

The month of November came and went and the holidays were fast approaching. Plans were made to meet on Christmas Eve day to start the festivities. Although the weather was brisk and cold, it stopped very few people from coming out to admire the trimmed shop windows.

The streets were full of bustle, with carolers singing, and people hurrying past, carrying brown paper packages and shouting greetings as they passed each other on the street. Little ones peered into the windows to glance one more time with hopes that Santa would fulfill their Christmas wishes. Church bells in the distance were chiming, "Silent Night" as Ken and Catherine enjoyed some last minute shopping.

At the corner of Center and Main stood Moyers Drug Store and Soda Fountain. It was a popular place and even busier than usual today. Although Mr. Moyer had a successful pharmacy, the store carried everything from "soup to nuts" and Catherine made it a point to stop in during the holidays to view the beautiful decorations and see the unique gift line that Mrs. Moyer had purchased for the season.

She was craving one of Mr. Moyer's chocolate malts. It had been a staple in the store for decades and competed on the fountain menu with their famous milkshakes. Fresh greenery hung over the archway. Pine wreaths on the front doors smelled so good and brought them back to seasons past. As they opened the front doors the shop owner looked up with a big smile and a nod. The couple found two free seats at the counter and ordered their ice cream treats. Mr. Moyer delivered the creamy concoctions himself and chatted for a few minutes. He was proud of the popularity of the malts they made. To give it that special taste, he always put just the right amount of malt powder in every time. Combined with vanilla ice cream, chocolate syrup and whole milk it was definitely a winner.

Soda Fountain

Joan Holman

The drugstore soda fountain dwells
In dim, nostalgic citadels.
This bustling hub is now passé,
A memory of another day.
 Beyond the bar, a mirrored wall
 Reflects the shiny knobs and all.
 Refrigerated boxes gleam,
 Their cavities filled with ice cream
For sundaes with cherry-topped dome,
And fountain drinks that fizz and foam,
For sodas, malteds, chocolate shake
While pausing on a shopping break.
 A rendezvous where old friends meet,
 A place to flirt and share a treat
 While perched atop tall stools that twirl
 As overhead, black fan blades whirl.
Or, seated in a private booth,
Swapping secrets, relishing youth.
Miniature juke box, close at hand,
With latest hits at our command.
 Sipping chocolate or cherry cokes,
 Exchanging all the latest jokes.
 In memory, I now retrace
 My steps to that familiar place
And linger midst my reveries
Of days and ways that used to be
Where the drugstore soda fountain dwells
In dim, nostalgic citadels.

TURN OF THE CENTURY DRUGSTORE
Lee Dubin, artist
Courtesy of the artist and Wild Wings, Inc.
Lake City, Minnesota

The snow began to fall as they headed to the Shaffer home to spend time with their loved ones. After hanging up their coats and removing snow clad boots they joined their family and friends. The flickering hearth warmed the house and the men had brought in ample logs to keep the fire burning. The music of the crackling wood brought comfort and relaxation and the sweet pleasure of being together.

With lots of introductions and warm wishes for a happy holiday, people gathered together to enjoy some goodies and cheer. Holly wreath pie, adorned with cut out leaves and berries, glistened with a rich red fruit filling. Centered in the middle of the table it was a tradition made by Ethel that had been enjoyed for years. Around it were Granny's gingerbread cookies, stuffed dates and sugared pecans. Custard like eggnog was served with cinnamon sticks and cream sherry was offered over ice or alongside a cup of hot coffee.

The couple worked the room, meeting new friends and reacquainting with others until it was time to head to the Christmas Eve service.

Their first holiday together was very special for the couple. The pair exchanged presents. Ken gave Catherine a silk, crepe floral scarf that was purchased from Kresge & Co. in New Jersey. It had a mauve and pink design with ribbon fringe. He opened a Parker 51 fountain pen from her. The burgundy writing instrument had a note attached with a humorous request to keep the love letters coming. The gifts were simple, yet something they'd treasure for years to come.

Time was spent cultivating their friendship. The desire to be trustworthy, considerate and loyal remained a constant, which came naturally as they cared deeply for each other.

From the beginning there was a degree of reserve, which showed respect, yet as their affection grew it became more difficult to keep those physical boundaries. Their love was genuine and Ken and Catherine agreed they had each found that special person to spend the rest of their lives with.

The miles between them strengthened the relationship. Conversations became more meaningful and they were able to share thoughts and feelings over the phone, cherishing the decision they'd made.

Ken and Catherine, 1950

~ 15 ~

The Engagement

With the holidays passing and the New Year off to a strong business start, Ken focused on his tool designing career, while making plans to purchase an engagement ring for Catherine. February was approaching and his plan was to propose on the fourteenth of the month.

Over the holidays, he'd made it a point to speak with her parents. Declaring his intentions, Ken asked Orval for his daughter's hand in marriage. They were delighted and he was given their blessings.

Being a traditionalist at heart, Ken wanted to surprise her with the ring, yet it needed to be the style that she loved. It would be worn daily and knowing Catherine, a day would not go by without her glancing down to admire and cherish the ring.

In determining his choice, he paid close attention to the jewelry she wore and also enlisted the help of his future sisters-in-law, Jackie and Nadine, as well as one of Catherine's closest friends, Poletime Comuntzis. Sworn to secrecy, they were only

Yasner & Sons Jewelers, 1957

too happy to provide their input. Between Jackie's drawings and a list of suggestions, the trio gave him excellent direction.

Back in Newark, he stopped in to see the family jeweler. Yasner & Son Jewelers on Green Street had earned the Corse family trust and business over the years due to their glowing reputation and the highest quality jewelry.

Mr. Yasner had known Ken since he was a boy and was only too happy to help. Since it would be a lasting and important symbol of their lifetime together, the jeweler listened carefully as Ken described in detail what he was looking for.

After several questions and some recommendations on clarity and carat weight, Mr.Yasner went to the jewelry cases. Based on the information provided as well as his years of experience in this field, he returned carrying a ring tray with several stunning pieces to view.

In the end, Ken played a significant part in the decision, and was grateful for the advice from people who knew and loved Catherine so well. Ken chose a classic style that would complement Catherine's skin tone. The round diamond was a stunning focal point and the smooth band would be comfortable on her delicate finger. After having the ring gift wrapped, he left the store with his purchase, ready to embark on the next chapter of their life together.

Valentine's weekend came quickly. The snow and icy weather took a break just in time for the travelers to make their way to Bloomsburg. The roads were clear for the most part, yet Catherine took her time when crossing the bridges, in case of slick patches. It was a bitter, cold day, with the mercury touching well below zero.

Her wool coat fit snugly, and the black beret and knitted gloves kept her warm. It was easy to take her mind off the winter weather because in just a few hours she'd be with her new love.

Her parents' home had become a perfect meeting place for the couple and Ken had made reservations for dinner at the Magee Hotel, where they'd had their first date. As she pulled into the driveway, she saw Ken had just arrived and was waiting. She hopped out of the car and smiled broadly. Their eyes met as they walked towards each other. "Welcome home, I've missed you!" "It's good to see you, too!" After a warm hug, they pulled back, eyes lingering and with smiles leaned in for a soft kiss.

As he took her suitcase she couldn't help but notice how excited he appeared to be, much more than usual. Was it just her imagination or did he have something in mind?

Many of Catherine's family had come in for a weekend visit and the house was filled with warm chatter. After dinner, the couple retired to the parlor to have some time alone together. The parlor was the favorite room in the house. There was nothing quite like getting cozy on a cold winter's night in front of the fireplace.

Catherine sipped her mug of mulled cider, while Ken added more wood to the fire. The crackling logs provided warmth and relaxation.

Ken had rehearsed this moment for weeks, yet his fingers trembled as he put his hand into the right pocket of his trousers. His heart jumped as he felt for the small box. The velvet case was right where it had been when he last checked a few minutes ago.

He reminisced as he laid eyes on her. "Catherine, my life has been so much better since I've met you. You inspire me with your patience and kindness, and I admire and respect you for so many reasons. I think we're on this "blueprint" together, and these are a few of the many reasons I'm hoping you'll want to spend our futures side by side."

Getting down on his knee, he opened the box. It was obvious by the look on her face; she was surprised and delighted at the same time.

Her heartfelt, "yes" came easily. "Of course I'll marry you! Was there any doubt?"

The proposal was private and the couple was able to share their real, unedited feelings. This soon changed. A full house of family and friends had come together ready to celebrate them and share their joy.

Gathering around the spinet – Catherine's Aunt Flossie sat down and tickled the ivories. Romantic tunes – "That's Amore" and "Because of You" by Dean Martin and Tony Bennett filled the air. The couple swayed back and forth to the music, as his hands rested on her waist and hers on his shoulders.

"Cake here, Drink there, Love Everywhere!" Handmade signs alerted the guests to a reception in the dining room where the cameras started flashing. These were fleeting moments moving enough to be captured on film... pictures that would live and move them forever and give the couple images to remember.

As the evening came to a close, "I Only Have Eyes For You" along with other favorite tunes could be heard on the Victrola and warmed the hearts of many on this cold wintry night.

"If I can't smoke in heaven, then I shall not go."

~ Mark Twain

Orval enjoyed his tobacco and his daughter's engagement was a perfect reason to bring out the cigars and Cognac. The men gathered on the front porch enjoying the rich tobacco of the Dutch Masters. The cigar burned evenly with every draw, throwing up puffs of cedar and spice aroma. Even the nonsmokers savored the scent. Puffing between hearty laughs, Orval was delighted to see his family looking so relaxed and happy.

The celebration was interrupted by the sound of bells jingling and snow crunching. Wrapped in shawls, the ladies emerged out on the porch to see a horse drawn sleigh making its way up Franklin Street. The single cutter sleigh was pulled by a Clydesdale. The horse was bay in color with white markings. Attending to the sleigh was a driver, dressed in top hat and cape.

Ken planned this private sleigh ride as an end to the evening. "Congratulations!" as the driver helped the couple onto the sleigh. The plush green velvet seats and the thick chase blanket allowed them to snuggle while enjoying the ride with comfort. The tin foot warmer filled with hot charcoal made their feet feel nice and toasty.

The sleigh lit by candle lamps offered enough light without taking away from the clarity of the night sky, and alerted others to the sleigh's presence.

The driver spoke to the horse in a clear and confident tone, and the sleigh pulled out, heading towards the center of town to take in the sights and sounds. It was sleek and light and built for speed. While the jingle broke the winter silence, the sleigh glided through a wonderland of snow.

Catherine kept feeling for the ring on her finger, deep inside her glove. It was still there, safe and sound. While the couple enjoyed each other's company, they took in the fresh air and sipped rich, thick hot chocolate.

The forty five minute ride took them through Bloomsburg. Passing by Carver Hall and the Courthouse was the Civil War Memorial. This was a special statue because it commemorated those who had served. The memorial lent grandeur to the town and Catherine's grandfather played an important part in helping to erect it.

The sleigh continued to pass through the diverse residential areas. Proud ownership of Victorian, Queen Anne and Colonial Revival homes stood tall, retaining integrity.

Cuddling in the back of the sleigh provided "talk" without words and with racing hearts they only had each other to focus on.

The sleigh stopped twice so that they could gaze up at the starlit sky, absorbing the silent winter night. The memorable sleigh ride was a perfect end to a romantic evening for the newly engaged couple.

Civil War Memorial

Wedding Bells

April 22nd, 1950

"Grow old along with me, the best is yet to be."

The Hudson was in pristine condition as it made its way through downtown Bloomsburg. Catherine's brothers rode in the front seat. As this was such a special day for the family, they made sure that the bride and father would be delivered to the church safely.

People waved and smiled as the automobile passed familiar businesses. The car looked impressive draped in white satin, the ribbon stretched to each side of the windshield forming a British V.

Catherine had plenty of room in the backseat as she sat next to Orval. The bride looked stunning in a gown of ivory moiré taffeta. The sweetheart neckline showcased a strand of pearls that Ken had given her at last night's rehearsal. Long sleeves ending in points over her wrists and a court train kept her warm on this chilly April day. Her fingertip veil of net fell from a beaded crown and as she glanced down at her feet she was happy with the decision she'd made. Wearing a pair of white kitten heels with folded bows, the shoes were comfortable, yet fashionable.

Catherine's bouquet was a special gift arranged by her father. The flowers consisted of white rosebuds showered with swansonia, pale peach sugar flowers and orange blossoms–all intended to promote love, marriage and fertility. Centered in the middle of the bouquet was a white orchid, which would serve as her corsage. Tucked next to the arrangement was her mother's prayer book.

The very Reverend Hunsicker met the couple at the altar and performed the ceremony.

After the reception in the social room, the newlyweds left on a wedding trip to the Poconos to start their life together.

Ken and Catherine, 1950

~ *17* ~

The First Years

 he couple settled into married life in Patterson, New
 Jersey where Ken owned a duplex on East 22nd Street.
Returning to his hometown and career at the Teterboro Air-
port proved to be the easiest transition.

They both worked hard at balancing career, love life, friends
and family, yet for Catherine this was a much bigger adjustment.
She took on a secretarial position which kept her busy by day.
Going from a suburban to an urban setting was difficult. The
commute and traffic was different from what she was used to.
Returning from a day's work, their row house, sandwiched in
with others, lacked sound proofing, and provided little privacy
for the newlyweds.

The backyard was tiny, and looking out at the small patch of
grass, Catherine missed her job and co-workers at the Department of Forestry and the great outdoor setting.

Before leaving Bloomsburg, Orval had given his daughter
a cutting of a special plant. A staple in her grandparent's flower

garden for years, the bleeding heart was divided and replanted at her parents' home when they were first married.

Catherine remembered the seedling had a prominent place in the backyard. Through the years its soft green foliage and bright pink flowers became a long time favorite. She closed her eyes and pictured her mother nurturing the plant. The heart shaped flowers hung in rows from arching stems and was one of her favorites. No matter how many times the plant was shared with family and friends, somehow it continued to survive.

Catherine found a partly shaded area by the patio, and with just enough space, carefully removed the perennial from the pot and planted it. The small bush required little care except for regular watering and promised to return every spring. A romantic flower, the bleeding heart became a treasured keepsake. It was a reminder of family and special times shared. She would re-create these same memories wherever they relocated, as it would later become all that she had left of her father.

Despite the differences, she chose to make the best of things and instilled the services of Ken to build a raised vegetable bed. In no time, the craftsman completed the planter made out of wood and filled it with soil. With fond memories of the family's homegrown harvest, the space was transformed from a bleak, limited setting into a colorful vegetable garden requiring minimal upkeep. The plants were nourished with a simple watering can and the enclosed garden made for little weeding. With the use of Catherines' green thumb, they were able to taste fresh vegetables once again.

Her mother's health was declining. Being the geographically furthest family member, Catherine did her best to keep in touch. Despite the distance, she made the long trek to Bloomsburg on a regular basis as she wanted to check in on her mother and do what she could to help. Every night she'd call home, a ritual that continued until her mother passed. The rest of the family ran errands, cooked meals, monitored medications and did housekeeping and kept Ethel company. Catherine was grateful for all that they did, yet she felt her contributions weren't enough and deeply wanted to be with her mother, especially during these last days.

Within a few years, their first child was on the way. After much consideration, the couple chose to move to the countryside. Loving the beauty and peacefulness, they felt the transition would offer a strong sense of community and provide a better quality of life.

By 1957, the family had grown to five with the addition of Carolyn, Kathy Ann and Kenneth Jr. Life was good but the move from urban to country had made for quite a financial hardship. Ken struggled to find a job that paid well. Employment opportunities in his field were limited. After relocating the family numerous times in hopes of finding the perfect home and job, he turned to temporary work.

For Catherine, she would no sooner get the household unpacked and in working order, than Ken would want to move again. Yet every place they lived, she made better than she found it. Tirelessly she cleaned and painted or wallpapered. If carpet was not afforded, the floors were covered with linoleum. Pretty plastic curtains hung from the windows in lieu of drapes. Outside, along with the children, she made sure the grass was cut and the garden tended to. She loved her children and provided the best care as a mother. Getting involved in church and community, the couple quickly made friends.

When Ken wasn't working, he spent hours daily creating inventions he was sure would bring in substantial earnings. The designs had to be flawless, with no room for error. Yet perfectionism was not profitable, and it took years to bring the plans to completion.

To bring in extra income Catherine took on several jobs working within the home. She advertised for ironing and would charge by the basket. Whistling away as clothes were pressed, she made the best of every situation. The children kept busy with books and craft projects, board games and stories and loved playing outdoors with their newfound friends. Dinner was made and served with love every night. She was thankful for the years spent in the kitchen with her mother and grandmother, learning to cook on a budget.

At night after the children were in bed, she'd set the typewriter out on the kitchen table. Taking on secretarial work, Catherine typed reports and letters into the wee hours of the night. The job was an added blessing as she could work from home and with a fourth child on the way, it would help tremendously.

Sadly, with all these efforts, they still lacked money needed for expenses. The savings account had long been exhausted and the temporary jobs that Ken had taken on offered no benefits. Christmas was coming and the heating bill would be due soon. As Catherine turned into bed, she lay awake contemplating what to do next.

~ *18* ~

Thanksgiving 1960

he once colorful autumn leaves had fallen and were now blowing around as Catherine made her way across Chestnut Street. The temperature had dropped and she was prepared for the weather. Between her favorite sweater, windproof jacket and corduroy slacks Catherine was nice and warm.

The expectant mother opened the door to her doctor's office. She was glad to have an early appointment as the waiting room was already filling with many pregnant women.

After checking in and taking a seat she stopped to catch her breath. This pregnancy was like the first three, yet the baby had been very active the last few weeks. She was trying to pace herself as she tired earlier in the day. She prayed for a healthy baby; a girl or boy did not matter to her. She would be delighted with either, although Ken was determined to have another son.

Her exam went quickly and Dr. Lubs felt the baby was right on target to be born in early January. Leaving the office, she was grateful that her good friend Skip was looking after the children.

It was the week of Thanksgiving. Original plans to celebrate in Bloomsburg had changed with the weekend forecast predicting wet and wintry road conditions. As they would be at their home for the holidays, Catherine made a stop at the grocery store. She pulled her list out, carefully written in teal ink for easy reading.

This would be a special Thanksgiving for the family. Several people had been invited to dine. A particular guest was George Robie, an assistant pastor of the church. He had relocated from the Boston area and quickly became their friend. The minister lived alone and because he had a limited salary, they often invited him over for dinner.

The invitations were important to George. His sweetheart, Marjorie still lived in Massachusetts, so the church family embraced George and soon became his second family. His love for the youth was obvious and the children flocked around him when he came to visit.

Catherine wasn't sure why, but she felt strongly there was a reason that George had come into their lives. What could it be? This sense never left her, especially when he was around. There had to be a reason. And soon she would find out.

As she left the store, she looked forward to Thanksgiving and what the future would hold. She prayed a better job would come along for Ken and that finances would improve. With their fourth and last child on the way, it would make things easier.

Thanksgiving proved to be a wonderful holiday. Gathering with friends helped take their minds off the financial burdens and to focus more on their blessings. One especially would be the birth of their child in just weeks.

For Catherine, her condition was good and she related this pregnancy to the others. Seeing Dr. Lubs on a weekly basis, he assured her that the baby was fine, and detected no problems.

With three other children to care for, Catherine was excited, yet eager for the baby's arrival. Trying to find a comfortable position to rest was getting more impossible with each passing day. Warm showers provided great comfort to her aching back and despite the discomfort, she was determined to keep a positive mindset.

She enlisted the help of the children which kept them engaged and together they did small tasks to get the nursery ready. The children felt important and much needed, and looked forward to the day when the baby would be brought home.

As Catherine and Ken were involved in several church activities, this would be Catherine's last month to teach church school for a while. She loved working with the children and it brought back fond memories of her days in Westfield.

As proud as the couple was, never letting on about their financial difficulties, the church was aware of the family's struggles and the ladies surprised Catherine with a baby shower.

Catherine was prepared to take a step back while others took care of things at home. Her dearest friends, Skip and Kitty, were ready and waiting for when the time came. Brother Richard and sister-in-law Eileen would be arriving to spend time with their nieces and nephew.

By early December, the lack of sleep combined with the baby's weight caused a constant feeling of exhaustion. Disappointed, Catherine realized she would need to stop her work until after the baby was born.

For Kenneth, he continued to search for the perfect job. With numerous interviews since summer, he was offered several opportunities. Yet the salary was not what he felt he was worth and he declined offers. Unemployment had kept the family afloat, yet would soon be coming to an end.

Catherine continued to be responsible for paying the monthly bills. This was not an easy task as the income could not cover the living expenses. Proud, she made every effort to maintain their good credit and worked with several establishments to pay the bills at a lower monthly rate. With the budget already tightened and extras long since cut, there were no more places left to trim. The new Chevy Belair station wagon had been sold and replaced with a much older model. An ad in the paper brought an interested buyer for their mahogany bedroom set purchased new from Magee's Fine Furniture in Bloomsburg. Oiled weekly and in pristine condition it would serve someone else beautifully for years to come.

The couple had also accepted an offer on the sale of their homestead. A big house and barn with plenty of acreage was replaced with memories. Renting a two family home from the Whitakers on Pierce Creek Road was a godsend. The landlords were amazed at how well-behaved the Corse children were and how clean and tidy Catherine kept the home. Loren and Barbara Whitaker soon became family and cared for the children like their own. Loren drove bus for the school district and would often take the children along for the afternoon run. As a nurse, Barbara checked in on Catherine regularly. Their older children, Lonnie and Judy, made great companions for the children. Having kind and caring neighbors helped to make this difficult transition so much better.

With the holidays getting closer and the baby's delivery approaching, George stopped to visit the family. That night, dressed as Santa, he brought a Christmas tree for the children. As Ken and George strung lights, the children waited patiently to add the ornaments. The fresh pine scent gave a special touch to the home and took Catherine back to Christmases past. After bedtime stories and tucking the tots in, George joined the adults downstairs.

Over coffee and dessert, the young minister could no longer contain his excitement. He would be asking Marjorie to marry him during the holidays. Still searching for that special ring he was sure he'd find one that he could afford. Prices were higher than he expected during the holidays, yet he would keep searching. The couple was happy for George and excited as Marjorie would be joining him in New York.

Catherine looked down at her engagement ring and memories flooded back to the night in December more than ten years ago when Ken had proposed. The ring had given her so much happiness and she never went a day without gazing at its brilliance and what it had meant to her.

After George left and the kitchen was in order, Catherine glanced at the Christmas list she'd made for the children. The presents would be small this year, very small. The bicycles would have to wait for now. She remembered Christmas as a child and how special her parents made the holidays, especially her mother. She would do the same. A purchase of red and white flannel was enough to make pajamas for all the children. Yet she wanted to be able to give them each one gift. Balancing the checkbook, they would be able to make do, although the fuel bill would have to be paid first.

With just two weeks left before Christmas, time was running out. Everything they could part with had been sold and in her condition, there was nothing that could be done in time for Christmas. Or was there?

As she gazed at the Christmas tree, and the soft twinkling lights, she asked for help. "Please God, send me a sign, please help our family this Christmas."

19

The Exchange

"Continue to be who and how you are . . . to
astonish a mean world with your acts of kindness."

~ Maya Angelou

The weather had been cooperative for her trip into town.
Ken had recharged the battery that morning and cleaned
the snow off the car. Out of work, she enlisted him to care for
the children while she went on an errand.

The night before she'd waited until the house was silent.
What she was about to do would be difficult enough let alone
having the children at her feet. Sitting by the brightly lit tree
she gazed down at the ring on her finger. The reflection of
the holiday lights gave an unusual sparkle to the diamond; it
was the last time she'd see it. It brought back memories of the
snowy night on Valentine's Day when Ken proposed to her.

She closed her eyes and envisioned the family gathering
round to celebrate the occasion. The sleigh ride through town
with Ken was like a fantasy and now it seemed so very long ago.

Things had changed; in some ways good, and in other ways not so good. She loved her husband, yet the financial strain made it difficult for her to feel close to him. There were jobs out there to be had, perhaps not the perfect one as he would like, but certainly any money coming in would take the pressure off their limited finances. Surely he could see the stress it had put on the family.

The suggestion to sell her ring had fallen on deaf ears and as the tears started streaming down her face she felt very alone and scared as to what the future would hold. She didn't want to part with the ring, yet there was nothing left of value that could be sold. It was all that she had.

Placing a finger on either side of the band, she slowly worked the ring down and over the knuckle, surprisingly coming off easier than expected. Worn daily for the last ten years, its absence would take some getting used to. The only reminder was an indentation which would disappear in time. Remaining on the ring finger was her wedding band. It would fill the void and symbolize their marriage together.

Going into the bedroom she opened the top bureau drawer. She knew exactly what she was looking for, as it had always been kept in the same place since they were married. Pulling back the sweaters, she took out a small tin and removed the lid. The papers were arranged just as they'd been back in 1950. Locating the paperwork from Yasner & Sons Jewelers, she gathered the bill of sale, appraisal, information on the clarity and size of the stone and the velvet box that held the ring. It was all there.

After cleaning the piece carefully, she took one last look before placing it inside its case. Tearfully, she shut the lid and put it in a bag along with the papers. The emotional evening had brought on a feeling of overwhelming fatigue. After placing a glass of water on the night stand, she laid back on the soft pillows and was asleep in a matter of minutes.

They had agreed to meet at a local diner across town. A family owned business for generations, the establishment was known for their home cooked breakfast. He was waiting when Catherine arrived. Her coffee had been brought to the table just as she liked it, with cream. She really wasn't hungry, but since she was eating for two, decided on a cup of oatmeal. The two friends chatted for a while and Catherine was relieved that she'd taken the quiet time last night to prepare for today. "The hardest part is over," she thought to herself.

He was more concerned for Catherine than his own circumstances. This was not the best time physically or emotionally for her to make a difficult decision. He asked again if there was any other way. She sadly shook her head, no. It was only after she insisted that the sale needed to happen that he agreed. He was familiar with the situation and was hesitant, yet very sympathetic. Had he been in a better place himself financially, he'd have made sure this didn't have to happen.

Looking at this humble woman who was ten years his senior, he was astounded at the depth of her love. In times of dark trial, when things were not going smoothly, she exemplified kindness and patience, generosity and tolerance. In his short years in the ministry, he saw she was a true blessing. The buyer had come to know and love Catherine as a dear friend and wanted to honor her wish. They talked for quite a while about his special lady and how much she would value and care for the ring.

Catherine was glad to know that the gift would continue on, taking a different path than was originally intended. She took comfort in knowing it would be worn by someone who'd cherish the ring as much as she did. Together they looked at the purchase. It would be a beautiful gift for his fiancée and the price Catherine had asked for was reasonable and affordable. The exchange was made and they each said their goodbyes.

As he watched her drive away, he vowed that she would never be forgotten, no matter how much time went by.

20

December 1960

"Our hearts grow tender with childhood
memories and love of kindred, as we are better
throughout the year for having in spirit, become
a child again at Christmas-time."

~ Laura Ingalls-Wilder

*D*ecember of 1960 proved to be a bitter one. With temp-
eratures dropping into the single digits and snow fore-
casts at an all-time high, Catherine was relieved, knowing that
there would be enough money for fuel to get them through
the winter months. Christmas had come and gone and the
children were happy with the presents they received.

The tree continued to be a focal point, as they played in
the living room. Beneath the twinkling lights Ken helped
the children set up their first Lionel train. The simple circular
track wove in and out around the bottom of the tree carrying
cars. His plans were to add on to the set each year, but for now
they were delighted with the new toy which kept the family
entertained for hours. She glanced at the train wishing her

family could be transported to another place in the same fashion. With the baby due any day, she missed her parents so much.

The bassinet sitting next to the tree had a prominent place in the main room of the home. This would be the fourth and last child to use it. The little bed was small, cozy and portable. Catherine wanted to keep the newborn close by and from previous experience, found it easier to lay the baby down, especially after childbirth.

Her suitcase had been packed for days and was sitting by the front door. Everything was in place and now they waited for signs to head to the hospital. Ken was certain the infant would be another boy—strong, gifted and able to carry on the Corse name. He already had great plans for the baby as he had with the other children.

As for the expectant mother, she was eager to know that the baby was fine. Like previous pregnancies, Catherine took good care of herself. Dr. Lubs was confident that she would deliver a normal, healthy baby. To her, that was all that mattered.

~ *21* ~

Chucky

Charles Wesley Corse came into the world on January 8th, 1961. Named after both of his grandfathers, their fourth and last child was destined to do great things. Ken was excited about sharing similar interests with both of his sons. He loved his daughters, yet the bond he'd already formed with his first boy would easily be duplicated with his second son.

As Ken and Catherine prepared the siblings for the arrival of the baby, "Chucky" quickly became the center of attention. The others easily adjusted to the newest member of the family and loved helping with whatever tasks involved the newborn.

Months passed and by the time Chucky approached his seventh month there were concerns. Catherine noticed the baby struggled to raise his head. As much as he tried, his attempts to sit up were impossible without help. As she watched him fight to roll from his back to his stomach with no success, she called the pediatrician.

Chucky, 1964

Nurse Gracie on the other end of the phone sensed the mother's anxious voice and scheduled Catherine and the baby in the urgency appointment section. The doctor had been a longtime friend and caregiver for the other children. As there was no sibling history of problems, he was confident that Chucky might be considered a slow starter. He took his time examining the baby and assured Catherine all was fine.

By the end of the first year, more concern brought another checkup. This time the medical team took a much closer look at the child's developments. With no attempt to crawl and lack of speech, a medical specialist was consulted for a second opinion.

The ride to Danville took close to three hours. The Chevy wagon was going on ten years old yet made the trip with ease. The heater worked well and with new snow tires on the vehicle, the couple felt safe and secure. Catherine was grateful that Ken agreed to come along. She'd packed with the intentions of staying for several days if need be. Two bags were filled with plenty of cloth diapers, formula, bottles, sleepers and more.

She took comfort in knowing the other children would be well taken care of. Her dear friend Skip and her daughters were only too glad to step in and help out. To the kids they were like family and looked forward to their company. The love and support from community, friends and family had been such a blessing and Catherine was very grateful, yet she still felt a sense of loneliness.

Glancing back at Chucky she smiled. He slept a good bit of the way looking so peaceful and content. Catherine knew her attachment to this little boy was even greater than what she had experienced with the other children. Fighting hard to control the tears, she blamed herself for the problems her son was having. Her health was a top priority all through the pregnancy. What went wrong?

It was difficult to talk with Ken about her concerns. He'd become annoyed with the whole situation, lashing out at her several times. If something was terribly wrong he would be devastated. Thankfully her father and siblings had been extra supportive, keeping in touch by phone in recent weeks and months. They'd be waiting at the hospital for their arrival. Months turned into years and the trip back and forth to Danville became a regular routine. Except for the seasonal changes the road traveled remained the same.

At the hospital, lengthy observations and testing took time. "Until the brain had reached full development, a complete diagnosis would not be given" was the explanation the doctors gave.

The medical team had come to love little Chucky and provided the best care possible. Friendly staff took time to listen to Catherine's concerns, offering helpful support and making sure that the baby was kept comfortable. Yet it was a frustrating process for the family and extremely upsetting for Catherine. At times, she questioned if the doctors really could determine what the problem was. She was well-informed, yet the definite developmental delays and abnormal growth concerned her.

Finally the time came when the results had been reached. Holding Chucky in her arms, they were given the grim news: "Your son has been diagnosed with Cerebral Palsy," said the doctor. Shock and disbelief took hold of the couple as the doctor told them he would never walk or talk.

Visibly shaken, they asked if it was possible that a mistake could have been made. Could any additional tests be done?

Sadly the doctor shook his head: "At this time there is no cure, and he will need much care. There are places for children like this if you can't provide for him."

It was such a vulnerable time and a very poor way for the doctor to deliver such shocking news. Catherine was overcome with grief and the nurse took Chucky from her arms. Weeping and sobbing, she shook with uncontrollable sadness and disbelief, which would continue for days.

Her precious son—what would she do? They had anticipated bad news, but not to this extent. Where would they go from here?

The more you give, the more you get...

The more you laugh, the less you fret...

The more you do unselfishly,

The more you live abundantly...

The more of everything you share,

The more you'll always have to spare...

The more you love, the more you'll find

That life is good and friends are kind...

For only what we give away,

Enriches us from day to day

~ Helen Steiner Rice

Mrs. Campbell

The next years were consumed with support and care for Chucky. The extended family pitched in and within no time had developed a network of people who offered all sorts of help. As a group, friends shared the delivery of meals and picked up the other children from school.

Day to day life took on a whole new meaning for the Corses. They had come to grips with the diagnosis and faced tough times. Yet, they refused to accept the doctor's final words. The 1960s opened what was once closed doors for the disabled. The Handicapped Children's Center accepted Chucky for physical and speech therapy. Appointments kept Catherine busy and with the help of her friends they were able to adjust to the long days. There were times when Catherine was physically and mentally exhausted, yet somehow she found the perseverance and strength to keep going and without a complaint. Carolyn, Kathy Ann and Kenny adored their little brother and carried him with them wherever they went.

Mrs. Campbell and Catherine, 2018

Mrs. Campbell, director of the center took a keen interest in Chucky. He was such a happy little boy despite the challenges he faced. She had much respect and concern for the mother. Catherine was pale and thin—she was well aware of the obstacles she encountered as she pushed forward with little support from the father.

During Chucky's therapy sessions, the director would offer Catherine a cup of coffee. The old percolator and the worn seats in the small office reflected her "open door" policy for family members. The handicap was treatable but incurable. It was not like a common cold. Delivering a pot of chicken soup would not make it all go away. But by offering an ear, a place to shed a tear or share whatever was on her mind on any particular day reminded Catherine that she wasn't alone.

The weekly visits with Mrs. Campbell made her feel less lonely and more hopeful. At times there was little conversation between the two women, yet the reassurance of support helped her to develop the strength and resilience she would need for years to come.

Catherine made it clear from the start that her son would never be isolated from family. She'd do whatever it took to help him learn and reach his potential and expressed her gratitude for the help they received. Routine visits connected her to others going through the same challenges, leading to new friendships and a shared sense of encouragement.

The staff felt privileged to work with such a dedicated parent and they all made sure that Chucky was given every chance for a better quality of life.

At the age of five, with assistance, Chucky took his very first steps.

~ *23* ~

Through the Years

Over time, Chucky would continue to prove the doctors wrong. After being carried for the first five years, he started to walk and talk. The change brought much joy to family and friends, except for Ken.

Following in his father's footsteps, Ken refused to accept anything short of perfection, including his youngest son. He expected the family to uphold the same standards. He divided time between temporary tool design jobs, wood working and creating inventions that were "certain to bring in much money." On occasions, he'd play with the other children, yet his actions spoke loud and clear. When it came to Chucky, it was Catherine's responsibility to raise him. Reflecting back on her own childhood, she was grateful and thankful for her upbringing. The sturdiness and work ethic she inherited as a Shaffer, along with her devout faith, sustained her.

To be available for her young son and the other children, Catherine acquired work in various ways. Her ironing services were offered at five dollars a basket. From little girls' dresses

The Corse family, 1962

to men's shirts, each piece was pressed carefully, building a loyal customer base. She took on housecleaning for families and at night her typewriter could be heard into the wee hours, completing work for a local appraiser.

Her day would begin at six o'clock with breakfast and coffee. During the summer months, she'd mow in the cool of the early morning. This was an enjoyable and mind settling task. As the push mower made its way around the yard, she watched the sun rise while listening to the chirping of birds. Catherine enlisted the children's help with a large vegetable bed.

"You don't have to garden, you get to," didn't always make them excited, yet they loved their mother very much and saw the effort she made. Canning and freezing the produce served them well through the winter months. Tales of bygone days helped pass the time and keep the children interested while preparing the vegetables. There was nothing like the taste of fresh picked green beans or peas.

On one summer afternoon, the day took a turn, and so did the weather. With a gust of wind swooping down on a pile of brush, a grass fire started, destroying acres of land. Several fire departments arrived to fight the flames. The next years' parcels were rich and fertile, yet Catherine would be remembered as "Smokey" for years to come.

Her father's love for flowers followed her as she developed quite a green thumb. Yellow marigolds, pink petunias and red geraniums filled the beds. Sawdust shavings kept the weeds away and added color very affordably. Removing her gloves, she'd often glance at her ring finger to make sure her jewelry was there, only to remember one ring was gone. It was a habit, even though the years had passed since she wore her engagement ring. Admittedly, she missed seeing the ring on her finger that once was there. It seemed like a lifetime ago when she sold her ring. Life had not been easy, yet it was meaningful. She sacrificed a material possession to take care of her family.

In the winter, they relied on coal to heat the home. Ken built a shoot which made deliveries into the cellar much easier. The large octopus furnace took over a good portion of the basement. Catherine would get up early each day to tend to the fire. She knew the routine well as she opened the vents, poked the embers, and added a thick layer of coal. By the time the children got up for school, the house was always cozy and warm, especially the kitchen. Through the cold winter months she would tend the fire throughout the day. Each night, before going to bed, the furnace would be banked by shaking down the ashes, emptying the ash pan and adding more coal.

After the children left for the day, she took Chucky to the school bus. There were so many folks only too happy to lend a hand. Catherine no longer had to carry her son up the stairs. She was concerned about making the bus late, but the friendly driver insisted Chucky walk the steps at his own pace, regardless of how long it took. At school, cafeteria workers helped carry his food trays until he mastered the task on his own. The day arrived and the workers were ecstatic for him!

Most importantly, his siblings grew up with a genuine kindness and compassion for others less fortunate.

Dinner time was family time and even when money was scarce, there was always a hot meal on the table. Catherine became "famous" by preparing certain dishes. Her sloppy joes and baked corn were Pennsylvania Dutch specialties that became a staple for generations to come.

GRAM'S SLOPPY JOES

1 lb. ground beef
1 cup ketchup
1 tablespoon yellow mustard
1 tablespoon brown sugar
1 tablespoon flour
1 teaspoon Worcestershire sauce

Brown meat and drain. Whisk together remaining ingredients and stir into ground beef. Simmer for 5 minutes. Serve over toasted rolls.

GRAM'S BAKED CORN

1 15oz. can of regular whole corn
1 15oz. can of creamed corn
1 egg, beaten
7/8 cup of milk
Salt and pepper to taste

Blend all ingredients and pour into greased 9X9 pan. Bake at 350 for one hour or until knife inserted in the center comes out clean.

During the school year, nightly homework was done at the kitchen table. It was an area of the home where Catherine could offer guidance and support to her growing children while studying lesson plans for Sunday church school.

Evenings included entertainment for the whole family. Lighthearted comedies provided good, clean fun, and science fiction shows kept all eyes focused on the television. The cost of a color model was out of reach, yet with three channels to choose from, a crystal clear signal from the rabbit ear antennas, and a swivel base, their black and white set was more than enough.

Weekends were a special time to invite friends over. Depending on the season, pastimes included ice skating, sledding, roaring campfires and board games, along with lots of sports like football, basketball, badminton and croquet to name a few.

Time was fleeting and soon the children turned into fine young adults. One by one, they "flew the nest," graduating from various colleges and starting careers. Dr. Kenneth Jr. was working in the medical field. Carolyn, a communications designer, was also a successful pianist and organist. Kathy Ann was employed as a dental hygienist and stayed close to home to be near her mom and brother. Taking a keen interest in occupational studies, Chucky started a small furniture refinishing business.

This gave Catherine some considerable flexibility. Despite the hardships endured, she had a most interesting life. By day, a secretarial position at the local university kept her busy and afforded them much needed health insurance. She also took up the hobby of oil painting. To Catherine, it was fun and rewarding and she enjoyed creating many works of art for her friends.

The family piano gave her great pleasure to play. Her favorite hymns "soothed the soul" and made her happy. It was an emotional outlet that relaxed and cheered her. And every day that she had the chance she spent it outside working in the yard.

Catherine was grateful for all the blessings that life had given her. Little did she know, another blessing was on its way. Something very special, something she never would have ever imagined was about to arrive in just a matter of days.

~ *24* ~

An Unexpected Surprise

"May kindness return to you in the same
beautiful way that it was given."

*I*t was January and the new year began with an historical storm. The Blizzard of 1996 made its way through
the northeast with wind-driven snow, paralyzing parts of the
country for days.

Thankfully, the weather predictions were announced in
advance, giving the aging couple plenty of notice to have
food and medications on hand. The last few months Catherine had been very busy. Ken was recuperating from a stroke
and required much care. The children and grandchildren had
made it a point to check in daily, and Dr. Kenneth Jr., was
consulting with the doctors on a regular basis to keep up to
date on his father's condition.

For Catherine, she looked forward to her daily exercise
outside. Close enough to check on Ken, the backyard offered
a perfect setting to make a snow covered trail. Although

the amount of snow had become a nuisance, it was also breathtaking. The quiet stillness and fresh air was a nice change for the 73-year old as she made strides on her cross country skis.

Coming in the back door, she smelled the aroma of hearty winter stew. Made early that morning, she'd filled the slow cooker with plenty of vegetables and beef. The smell of onions and carrots triggered her appetite. Hopefully the family would make it over for supper. Crusty bread, salad and apple crisp, along with the stew would be a perfect meal on a cold snowy night.

After giving Ken his medications, she headed back to the kitchen to prepare lunch. "The Price is Right" would be airing soon and they enjoyed watching their favorite show while eating their noon meal. The kids had pitched in and together purchased their father a lift recliner. The chair offered support, while the push of a button helped bring him to his feet. Between the use of a walker and rehabilitation, the 77-year old was starting to make progress slowly as he made his way across the room.

The family was supportive as well as concerned... not only for their father, but more so for their mother. Although she never complained, they could see the responsibilities of caregiver were taking a toll.

Of all four children, it was Chucky who checked in the most. As he sat next to his father, he'd talk and hold his hand. The unconditional love he received from his special needs son, reached deep down inside of him and softened the old man's heart, changing the direction of what his last years would be like.

Catherine had been working on a jigsaw puzzle when the doorbell rang. With the weather so severe the last few days, she wondered who could be out in these conditions? Perhaps it was the minister, coming to pay Ken a visit.

She peered through the frosted glass and saw Don. Dressed in a trapper's hat with a big scarf, she almost didn't recognize their postman. Braving the frigid cold, Catherine opened the door and invited him in, while she ran to get a thermos of piping hot coffee.

He visited with the couple for a few minutes, then took out the mail as well as a package. The parcel was addressed to Catherine and required a signature confirmation. After acknowledging receipt, the carrier thanked them for the warm up and left to make his last deliveries for the day.

"It is said that a letter from the heart
can be read on the face of the recipient."

Catherine didn't get many deliveries and certainly wasn't expecting any today. It wasn't her birthday or any other special occasion. She also didn't recognize the return address on the parcel. Whoever prepared the box had gone to great lengths to make sure it was wrapped properly. Every seam was reinforced with packaging tape to assure a safe delivery.

After opening the package, she took out an envelope with her name on it. The box was filled with lots of cushioning material and an extra label. She was certain whatever was inside must be very important.

She slid the opener across the top crease of the envelope and pulled out the contents. Starting to read the letter, the women's eyebrows raised. Her mouth dropped open as she continued to read the letter. With legs weakened, she found a chair and sat down in disbelief.

The letter was dated January 3rd, 1996.

Dear Catherine,

It makes me very happy to be able to return this to you after all these years. George knew I wanted to do this, so he gave me another for Christmas. I always felt badly that you had to give it up, but can understand why. I hope I've taken good care of it. Please wear it with much love.

Marjorie and George

By now Ken had joined her. With trembling hands, she reached deep inside and took out a small box. It was labeled "Yasner & Sons Jewelers," Newark, New Jersey. After lifting the lid, she gasped. She couldn't believe her eyes! There was her engagement ring! Although many years had passed, the memories returned to Valentine's Day of 1950, when Ken had proposed, giving her the ring. Along with it was the original bill of sale and paperwork dating back to February 4th, 1950.

A warm glow spread across her face as she held the ring. It was still such a beautiful piece. The stone had its same brilliance, and the shiny gold band looked brand new. Some 36 years had passed since she had removed the ring from her finger. Arthritis had set in. Would it still fit?

The elderly man reached out and took the hand of his bride. Glancing down, the once soft and youthful hand had aged so much over time—a hand that had done so much for so many. Yet it was more beautiful than ever. With tears of joy, she watched as Ken placed the ring on her finger. Sliding over the knuckle, it once again had a prominent place on her hand.

On that day, an angel "earned its wings" as Catherine's countless acts of kindness and generosity had returned to her. This gift was given for no apparent reason but love. Although it made Catherine extremely happy, thoughtful and generous giving had rewards. For Marjorie and George, the selfless act of kindness was gratifying. As they had so much respect and admiration for Catherine, it was their true desire to return the ring to its rightful owner.

"Taste and see that the Lord is good.
Oh, the joys of those who trust in him."
Psalm 34:8

Catherine, 2016

*Catherine at her
95th birthday party, 2018*

~ *25* ~

An Abundant Life

"Those who act kindly in this world will have kindness"

*T*he compelling journey of my mother's ring is one of many examples of how she has chosen to live her one remarkable story.

At the time of this writing mom just celebrated her 96th birthday where she received over 100 cards from friends and family! It gives me so much joy to share with readers what she's doing today. The book has been a gift to her from my heart... a testament of my love and my great honor to write.

Mom's life has been one of abundance. Yet, what is an abundant life? Naturally, one might think it's a life filled with financial wealth, although it's not about the money. Her abundance in life comes from love, service and caring for others. It's about being connected—to friends, to family and to community. Mom is definitely connected!

If an abundant life consists of true friendships then mom has been blessed tenfold. Those who know her love her, and those who don't, want to. A recent visit to the hospital for emergency surgery left the team of doctors and nurses stunned. "Your mother is an inspiration," "I've never met anyone quite like her" and "I can't believe she's 96 years old!"

She has a following wherever she goes. Kate, Kitty, Aunt Cass, Mom, Gram, Aunt Kate, Cathy, Shorty and Kacky are some of the many names she's been called. With fondness, I refer to her as "St. Catherine."

While sitting at the computer typing, I just spoke with this angel. She's off to work at the CHOW pantry, where she assists in filling food orders. Chances are, you won't find her at home, at least not until spring. Instead, she'll drive a friend to a doctor's appointment or pitch in with the local community dinner. Her daily routine includes a stop at Chuck's to pay him a visit.

Brownies and cookies made with love are a staple. They're found at the Election Day bake sales, coffee hour or for someone who just needs a pick me up. Holding a secretarial position at church, she takes notes for board meetings and has influenced the lives of many young people through her decades of teaching church school.

Today, she resides with my sister Carolyn and brother-in-law, James. Their beautiful home consists of an in-law suite with plenty of space for mom, another generous act of kindness. She has her own designated parking spot and still drives a 1993 Toyota, the last car she and dad owned together.

The feeders outside her deck are filled with food for her bird friends. Using a BB gun, her accurate shot hits the squirrel targets easily. When it snows, she'll work alongside her family with a little electric blower, keeping the driveway and walkways clean.

Jigsaw puzzles always have a prominent place in her living room and she loves company to help finish them. Her Kindle reader is packed with books to read and games to play and this little firecracker is an avid NFL and UCONN basketball fan. Dare to challenge her in a game of double solitaire! You won't win.

Surviving the Great Depression, it amazes me how much pride mom takes in whatever she has no matter how humble. Her home is tidy and clean and the "waste not want not" attitude has made me think twice about how precious our resources are, such as running water, electricity and heat. I remember as a child we were recycling long before it became the thing to do. Mom was ahead of her time!

Catherine, 2018

As the warm weather arrives, the garage door opens, and with the roar of an engine out comes mom on the riding lawn mower! She's upgraded to a riding machine and loves to maintain the yard. By fall, an attachment is added as she toots around collecting all the fallen leaves. Listen carefully and one will hear the faint whistling over the mower. She is so happy in the great outdoors.

The hobbyist is only too happy to provide tours of her flower garden. Filled with perennials and annuals, this special place beautifies the yard and serves as a welcome retreat for many of Catherine's bird friends. Nature's beauty is soothing and creates a calming influence for all who stop by for a spell, including the 96-year old gardener.

On display in a prominent place is the favored plant. Nurtured and loved for decades, you will see the bleeding heart plant. That's right! The same flower that was given as a gift by her father on her wedding day! Traveling for 68 years and relocating over 15 times, it has reached its final resting place, quite happy and content.

Jordan, Catherine and Kaitlyn, 2017

When people inquire about the grandchildren, she'll light up like a Christmas tree. "If pride is a sin, I'm guilty!" she'll say, and proceed to tell you all about Kaitlyn and Jordan.

Our dear friends, Pam and Jimmy, own a property near the beach on Sanibel Island, Florida. Over the years, they have graciously made their house our home, with a trip the family looks forward to every year.

"Gram" is the best part of the vacation. She's found her piece of paradise and is certain: "Heaven will look just like Sanibel!" Days are spent walking the sugar sand beaches. An avid shell collector, she carefully washes and dries her finds every night of the trip and her mesh bag is filled with treasured seashells to take back home.

Catherine at the beach in Sanibel, 2015

From pelicans to seagulls, to little sandpipers that scurry along the water, Gram gets her fill of bird watching and keeps track of all of her sightings. She enjoys a beach picnic under the big umbrella and the rest of our time is filled with fun memories to last a lifetime.

Catherine at the beach in Sanibel, 2015

People often ask: "What do you attribute your long life to?" Her answer is always the same: "prayer and lots of coffee!"

Over time one of the many things I've witnessed was my mother's faithfulness to daily prayer. Her faith and devotion to God was and is still unwavering. Her commitment to church tithing, even when there was very little to give is an inspiration to me. "You can't outgive God," she says and continues to support a child every month from a third world country.

As times have changed over the years the one thing that has remained constant is my mother's love. To really test the depth of someone's love, take a look at how kind, how patient, how generous, how tolerant that person is in all sorts of situations. In times when things are not always the smoothest, but rather in challenging, difficult times.

The memories of her love for me and for my siblings are endless, yet one always resonates in my mind.

Catherine and Kathy Ann, 2016

While in junior high school, "Spirit Day" was going to be held on Friday. Everyone was supposed to wear something blue and gold to school to show their support. I owned a gold turtleneck, but nothing blue. Mom knew the situation. It was Friday morning when I woke up and saw the most beautiful blue vest and skirt. Looking closely at the pretty fabric, it was very familiar. I'd seen this before. It was then that it dawned on me. Mom had taken the material from one of her dresses to make my outfit.

Chucky, 2018

For many who have asked about Chucky, he turned 57 this year and lives in a bungalow with his kitty, a short distance from the family. He keeps active in woodworking and is enrolled in a program through a wonderful organization called Springbrook. They work with Chucky to achieve personal goals and take him on social outings. He looks forward to a yearly Caribbean cruise with his traveling friends. His favorite foods are still pizza and hamburgers and someday he hopes to see Disney World. Chucky taught us that loving someone is not about what we want them to be, but about who they are.

It was on our father's deathbed that Chucky finally heard the words, "I love you, son."

~ 26 ~

All That I Had:
A Daughter's Reflection

"Don't be afraid of dying, be afraid of an unfulfilled life."

The concept of a life of service sounds like a wonderful idea, yet where does one find the time for these "random acts of kindness?"

Feeling the same way, and witnessing the positive influence mom had in my life and in the life of so many others, I had a burning desire to follow in her footsteps. Yet the disease of being too busy (or "dis-ease") interfered with our family. As a single parent it was important to be fully present with my children and the people I loved and cared about. How could I take time to serve others with an already overloaded schedule?

Robert Byrne said, "The purpose of life is a life of purpose." This is what I craved! Through developing a much simpler way of giving "All That I Had," life took on a whole new meaning. Starting with small gestures that lifted other people's spirits, it quickly became apparent that these random acts required little effort on my part. It turned into the highlight of my day, and although I could see the positive impact on others, the concept honestly did more for me than for them!

They say that a habit takes 30 days to form and it is years later that Operation "All That I Had" is in full swing for me, so much so that I'm excited to share some of my findings and helpful tips with all of you.

Warning: This program will bring out a smile, warm the heart and is "contagious." Once you "catch" it, it's hard to stop and will stay with you. It's guaranteed to improve well being and is life-changing for all involved!

Here are some of my favorite acts of kindness, ones I've used for years:

1. **Give positive feedback.** If you had great service in a restaurant, store or even online, it takes just a moment to let someone know. Recently we had lunch at a local restaurant and the server was wonderful. At the end of our meal I asked to see the manager. After giving a great review, the server returned relieved, thinking at first we had complained. She told us our compliment made her day!

2. **Send a Card.** I call this the "Power of One." Every day send one card to someone to make their day. Invest in some boxed cards and postage stamps. You'll be amazed at the response! PS: If you miss a day or two, no worries. You can send an extra card another day. I often do this while waiting for an appointment or in between other tasks. Card ideas: Thinking of you, someone who lost a loved one or friend, birthday, a person going through a difficult time, a recipient

who just received an award or promotion, appreciation or gratitude, and just for no reason at all.

3. **Purchase some one dollar lottery tickets.** Hand one to the person who takes your ticket as you exit the parking lot, or someone who made extra effort in wrapping a bouquet for you. The possibilities are endless! A ticket popped in a card saying "you're worth a million!" is sure to please!

4. **When writing an e-mail.** Give a word of encouragement, a thanks, or to wish someone a great day–it will make it a great day for them!

5. **Open a door for someone with a smile.**

6. **Give someone the chance to go ahead of you in line.** Let a car out in front of you in traffic. If someone returns the favor, be sure to wave as you pull out!

7. **Give a sincere compliment.** "I love your scarf" or "Your dress is so pretty." I know how much it meant to have someone tell me "Your children are so well behaved" when we were out in public.

8. **Share a meal by cooking a little extra.** Our next door neighbor, Charlie is 90 years old and lives alone. He enjoys any food we deliver. It's easy, and the smile on his face is worth every minute to walk it over!

9. **No time to cook? No problem!** Take a meal to someone in need. Many of the grocery stores have

delicious, ready to go entrees. If you have time, sit with the person and have a slow conversation.

10. **Remember our four-legged friends.** After 16 years, we recently said goodbye to our cat, Seffie. She was part of our family. We adopted another kitty, who needed a good home. If you can't have a pet, many organizations can always use spare blankets, sheets or towels as well as dry food for the animals or someone to visit–give them some love.

11. **Invest in a porch swing.** Looking for time to stand still? Even for a few brief moments? It's been over 50 years, yet the memories of Grandpa's porch swing whisked me back to a much simpler life.

Two years ago we installed a swing on our front porch and here's what we discovered:

⋆   A simple, magical quality comes over anyone who sits there.

⋆   Quiet conversation and laughs replace cell phones.

⋆   The porch comes alive with discussions, stories and songs.

⋆   People walk away happier.

⋆   Friends ask if they can come over and swing, even if we aren't going to be home.

⋆   Fast-paced life and pressures are replaced with more carefree moments.

No porch? Swing stands are available for your deck, patio or yard.

12. **Make a Memory Bag.** This is a real winner! Type up one or two sentence memories or words of appreciation for someone special. Cut apart each memory and put them in a small gift bag. The recipient is supposed to read one memory a day but chances are they won't be able to wait! My children made me a memory bag years ago, some thoughts made me laugh, others brought tears and then some memories I had forgotten. I still read the notes from time to time.

13. **Take a picture every day for a week.** Every day take one picture of something or someone you're grateful for. At the end of the week, scroll back and count your blessings!

14. **A gift that keeps on giving.** A while ago my hair stylist lost her mother. She was so special to Tracey. I purchased a vase for her to keep at the salon and occasionally will drop by with flowers to help keep her mom's memory alive.

15. **Give things away for free on Craigslist**

16. **Send an e-mail prayer.** For those who believe in prayer, I love this pick me up. I've often sent a prayer to someone by e-mail who is going through a difficult time. As my children don't live locally, it's another way to reach out sooner and let them know how much they're loved.

17. **What's a special talent that you have?** For example, by sharing your skills such as cooking, writing, planning an event, fixing or repairing something, or even lending an ear to a friend in need, it could really make someone's day! The possibilities are endless.

Albert Schweitzer said it well: "I don't know what your destiny will be, but one thing I do know; the only ones among you who will be really happy are those who have sought and found how to serve."

Performing simple acts of kindness or gratitude can bring benefits for years to come. Don't wait for the opportunity to be of service, go out and create them!

Kaitlyn and Catherine, 2016

It is Catherine's wish that at the time of her passing, for her engagement ring to be given to her granddaughter, Kaitlyn. Catherine's desire is for Kaitlyn to care for the ring and to continue on sharing this one remarkable story.

A portion of the sale proceeds of this book will be given to the organization "Helping Celebrate Abilities" formerly known as the "Handicapped Children's Association" in memory of Mrs. Ann Campbell.

About the Author

For years, Kathy Corse has been known as a well-respected, business developer in sales, leadership and customer service. A highly skilled executive and opportunity driven, Kathy generated millions of dollars in sales yearly, and assisted corporations in sales force and revenue growth.

She became a master team builder, mentor and coach, adept at teaching and motivating others and planned events that delivered results. Priding herself in the best customer service, she developed a large and loyal client base and was trusted and respected by her peers.

Her wealth of knowledge and dynamic speaking ability, coupled with her warm, genuine and winning personality, made her a sought- after keynote speaker at conferences where she regularly spoke to audiences of thousands of people.

Despite her resounding success, what really defines Kathy is her kindness, enthusiasm and genuine desire to make a difference in the life of every single person she meets.

Upon retirement Kathy spent more quality time with her mother. By recording adventures, going on outings, and asking questions, she gained rich information about her family. Her long time dream turned reality with the authentic and inspiring completion of her first non-fiction novel, "All That I Had." By making a positive and meaningful difference in her writing, she's excited about connecting with her children, relatives, readers, and future generations to come.

Residing in Upstate NY and business owner of "My Grandpa's Hudson", Kathy offers chauffeur driven rides in an expertly restored 1951 Hudson, similar to what her grandfather drove. In addition, she gives oncology drives to folks heading to appointments, hoping to brighten their day.

Kathy is available for select speaking engagements.
To inquire about a possible appearance, please contact:

KathyCorse@gmail.com